9781570082535

Fathering

Fathering

Matthew Richardson

Bookcraft
Salt Lake City, Utah

Library of Congress Catalog Card Number: 96-84619
ISBN 1-57008-253-7

First Printing, 1996

Printed in the United States of America

To my family—
      with devotion and love.

Contents

1

"Congratulations, Dad!"

I guess there are some things in life that, try as you might, you just can't imagine . . . *accurately*. For example, my wife and I had the opportunity to travel to Switzerland. We were excited to see the famed Matterhorn. Whenever I tried to imagine standing at the foot of the Matterhorn, I saw Disneyland. I had visited Disneyland on several occasions, so I knew the Matterhorn (and the bobsled) well. As we rode the train to the tiny town of Zermatt, located at the base of the Matterhorn, my excitement grew. I closed my eyes and imagined Lisa and myself standing at its base. There we were, standing in a field smothered with wild flowers with climbers waving as they walked past to embark on their mountaineering conquest. I even heard the faint bellowing (in stereophonic sound, no less) of the "abominable howl" that I had grown to love/hate in the caverns of the Disney Matterhorn.

Upon our arrival in Zermatt, after a short walk we stood and viewed the Matterhorn. I was taken aback by the beauty. It was so different from what I expected. It was better . . . it was *real*.

By the way, there isn't a bobsled ride or abominable snow monster on the *real* Matterhorn (just in case you were wondering).

As happened with the Matterhorn, I have found that my perception of reality often doesn't agree with reality. I remember when my wife first told me she was pregnant. Both she and I were full-time college students, working three jobs between us and struggling to make ends meet. I remember standing in our tiny basement apartment, complete with plumbing for decoration, when my wife broke the news. "I'm pregnant!" she said in excitement. *Pregnant?* my mind questioned. I asked her to call the hospital back and double-check the lab work. "Congratulations, Dad," she said as she hung up the telephone receiver.

Congratulations, Dad? I was excited, but I couldn't get the word *dad* to stop ringing in my ears. *Dad?* My mind raced. Although I looked forward to the experience and even anxiously anticipated it, there was something deep down inside me that was screaming: "You . . . a dad?" How could I possibly be a dad? I didn't even have any power tools! Amidst the mental confusion, there was one comforting thought in the back of my mind: I knew that I had a little time to prepare for the experience. Nine months. At the time, nine months seemed like such a long time. I reasoned that a good contractor can build a house or two in nine months, so surely I could figure out fatherhood in nine months.

Nine *short* months later (it is easy for me, or anyone else who has never been pregnant, to say "nine short months"), I found myself in a situation oddly similar to—yet profoundly different from—the Matterhorn adventure I described earlier. As I stood in a delivery room at the regional medical center, I nervously watched as my wife prepared to deliver our firstborn child. I had viewed the birthing videos, read the pamphlets, and attended the delivery classes at the hospital. I had even memorized all the breathing techniques: panting, "hee-hee-phew," and the final command—"push." I had imagined this day for the past nine months, but my perception of delivery day had not been quite the same as what I was now beholding. This was reality.

I tried to think where those nine *long* months of preparation went. This reminded me of tests I used to take in elementary and secondary school. "This is a test," the proctor would say in a monotone voice. "You have exactly six minutes to finish this section. Pick up your pencils and begin [there was always a long pause]—now!" I would feverishly read, figure, and mark the answers I knew. Then I would go back and guess at the questions I didn't know. After all, the proctor told us that "there is no penalty for guessing." In what seemed more like two minutes than six, the proctor bellowed: "Stop! Time's up. Lay your pencils down." It was unnerving to lay a pencil down when I didn't know all the answers or had been forced to wing it because of the time constraint.

Now I stood in a delivery room with a knot in my stomach and throat, dressed in a flimsy paper suit (complete with booties, mask, and hat that resembled something a far-out painter from France would wear). I could just hear the voice: "Stop! Time's up. You are now a dad." I must admit that reality is often somewhat overwhelming. I couldn't help but recall that well-used cliché, "When the opportunity arises, the time for preparation is past." Since I ran out of time preparing, I supposed I could always guess at or wing fatherhood. As with those timed tests, hopefully there would be no penalty. Yet somehow guessing seemed out of the question. Nine months before, I was certain I would be prepared to be a father, but now my confident statement that "anyone can prepare to be a dad in nine months" came back to haunt me.

What I witnessed in that delivery room was truly a miracle. I was stunned, overwhelmed, overjoyed, and fearful all at once.

I honestly never knew I was capable of the depth of feeling I experienced at that time. It was better than I had imagined. This most memorable and striking experience, however, brought everything to a grinding "reality check" when a masked nurse handed me a small, bundled baby boy and said, "Congratulations, Dad!" Déjà vu! My mind raced again. *Dad!?* This time I was actually holding *my* son. How could I be a dad? I *still* didn't have any power tools!

2

The Visions of Fatherhood

Every father must grapple with the perceptions of fatherhood. What has continued to amaze me, however, is that so many fathers have hardly given fatherhood a second thought, let alone prepared for it. Herein lies a great irony. We spend most of our lives in preparation or training for something. Young teens spend hours studying, practicing, and begging for hands-on application in preparation for a profound event: receiving a driver's license. You don't find too many teens who have to be forced to practice driving a car, backing it out of the driveway, or just starting it up. But when it comes to preparing for the significance of parenthood—forget it! Many parents find that we pour more energy into our professions than into our families, pore over our banking statements more than over our children's report cards, and spend more time in meetings than at dance recitals, school plays, or sporting events where our children are participating. To practice a professional vocation, we must almost always be licensed. To be a parent, on the other hand, you hardly have to do anything. You aren't required to read a pamphlet, attend classes, or pass an exam. Something is horribly wrong in a society that diverts our attention to things on the periphery and keeps us busily engaged in things of less significance than our families. You might say we are "in the thick of thin things."

What Does Fatherhood Mean?

If we hope to become better fathers, it is important that we understand what fatherhood *really* is. If our perception of an event is not accurate with reality, we find we are inadequately prepared. When it comes to fatherhood, many of us don't completely understand what is expected of us. We toddle along, winging it or living up to our preconceived image of fatherhood. What exactly is a father or fatherhood?

There are many names for fathers: dad, papa, father, the old man, etc. Many dictionaries define a father as a "male parent." However, most of us are not driven by definitions but by expectations, roles, perceptions, and previous experience. Our perspectives about fatherhood's definitions and roles are generally shaped by our experience with fathers. Without being aware of how we conceive of fatherhood, we may continue to act out our preconceptions of fatherhood without considering other possibilities. Some of the most significant types of fathers that influence our perception of fatherhood include "household fathers," "image fathers," "public fathers," "ecclesiastical fathers," "absent fathers," "divine fathers," and "priesthood fathers."

The Household Father

One common thread connecting all of mankind is the fact that each of us has parents. Granted, not all parents are participatory, present, or available, but every individual has natural parents—two of them! Through our association (or lack thereof) with our own parents, most of us begin to shape our conceptions of parenthood. Therefore our earliest perception of fatherhood is linked with the experiences we've had with our own fathers. A myriad of images—both good and bad—are gathered through our personal experience with our own fathers.

The Image Father

Social influences can have a dramatic effect on our perceptions. Image fathers are idealized fictionalizations established according to the social image of the day, culture, or location. You never actually meet an image father in real life. Fathers portrayed in film, television, greeting cards, church lessons, or Father's Day sacrament meeting talks qualify as image fathers.

I distinctly remember the Cary Grant image of fatherhood. Cary Grant's movies usually portrayed the main character as a successful businessman (usually company president or a high-ranking executive), older, established, and owner of a spacious home and a nice car or two. Possessing all the comforts of life, he begins dating. Eventually he gets married, has children, and lives a comfortable life. I was influenced by the Cary Grant father image in that I always imagined that by the time I was a father I would have certain things. For example, my first fatherly thought was about owning power tools. Luckily for me, however, this image was not my only basis for judging what fatherhood was supposed to be like—otherwise I would have been doomed because I lacked a real job, a corporate title, a spacious home, and the cars.

Other media influences that create image fathers include television shows such as *Leave it to Beaver, The Courtship of Eddie's Father, My Three Sons, The Brady Bunch,* and many current daytime and prime-time dramas. Print advertisements in family publications portray the family in picture-perfect settings with the father dressed in designer labels or casually lounging with every hair in place. On the other hand, the image fathers portrayed on today's talk shows would make Cary Grant retreat in bewildered paranoia. The image father is portrayed in isolated snippets of what America perceives everyone else's dad is really like.

The Public Father

While no one ever meets an image father, every child is exposed to public fathers in one way or another. Public fathers are real men, not media images. Public fathers can be famous or nefarious. They range between the coolest dad on the block or in the ward to a dad so dumb the thought of him makes his children's eyes roll and heads bob as they describe him. For some kids, it seems that every public dad is cool except their own dad in public.

Children observe public fathers in action as they eat with their families at McDonald's, walk the malls, stroll through a grocery store, work at home, play ball on the front lawn, or take family vacations. Public fathers are Little League coaches, Scout leaders, youth advisers, and teachers at school. For the most part, these are the men who will grease the squeaky wheel, provide sanity to an insane world, teach America how to catch, show deacons how to pass the sacrament and earn merit badges, attend daddy-daughter dates, chaperone every stake dance, and generally be there when nobody else is.

Unfortunately, public fatherhood is generally a one-dimensional image. We observe the public side of fathering, but we have difficulty connecting that image with the private, everyday role of fatherhood. Like the image father, the public father can be dangerous because many children will expect their household fathers to act like image or public dads in private settings.

The Ecclesiastical Father

In a way, the ecclesiastical father and the public father are very similar. Both types of fathers can be observed in public, but the ecclesiastical father is seen only in amiable church settings (except during church basketball games, when Brother Jekyll sometimes turns into Mr. Hyde). Church fathers are seen at a friend's family home evening, as bishops, or in other church callings. You can find them sharing an experience, taking time to talk, teaching values and Sunday School lessons, and maybe even getting choked up occasionally when something really important comes up. Unless one's household father is also an ecclesiastical father, church dads provide some people with their only experience of family prayer, a priesthood blessing, or a testimony borne by the Spirit.

Whatever our perceptions about them might be, fathers are real and vital. Whether from personal experience, a dictionary, public observation, or the media, we formulate images of fatherhood. The role of fatherhood, however, is shifting.

The Absent Father

In a recent publication, David Blankenhorn, a noted author on the topic of fatherhood, wrote, "Over the past two hundred years, fathers have gradually moved from the center to the periphery of family life" (*Fatherless America: Confronting Our Most Urgent Social Problem* [New York: Harper Perennial, 1995], p. 13.) I don't believe that Blankenhorn's concern is that fathers are no longer in the limelight or on center stage. His statement is not possessive or about control. It does, however, sound an alarm of a potential danger. The danger lies in the periphery. When you look at a photograph, for example, you will notice that things in the periphery are out of focus, blending in with the scenery. If Mr. Blankenhorn is correct, fathers are blending into the scenery of life and will eventually become nonexistent altogether. Unfortunately, for many families a father's disappearance is more of a reality than a feared future event. In repeated national studies, researchers are finding that fathers are becoming nonexistent in familial roles.

Even more disturbing are the possible effects on the fatherless. There are literally thousands of pages of research that detail the current problems of children approaching adulthood. Society is reeling in disbelief and denial as we find a strong link between crime and single-parent families. Furthermore, fatherless daughters are 53 percent more likely to marry as teenagers, 111 percent more likely to have children as teenagers, 164 percent more likely to have premarital sex, and 92 percent more likely to dissolve their own marriages (see I. Garfinkel and Sarah S. McLanahan, *Single Mothers and Their Children: A New American Dilemma* [Washington, D.C.: Urban Institute, 1986]; see also K. Zinsmeister, "Do Children Need Father?" *Crisis,* October 1992, pp. 31–33). The absent father impacts economics, reading, self-esteem, work ethic, moral values, sexual identity, and more.

A memorable editorial caught my attention a few years ago. In a popular news magazine, the headline read, "Dear Dads: Save Your Sons." The article was written by a psychologist who was counseling a troubled teenage boy and his distraught mother. It was the author's concluding comment that caught my attention and gripped my soul: "I have come to believe that most adolescent boys can't make use of professional counseling. What a boy can use, and all too often doesn't have, is the fellowship of men—at least one man who pays attention to him, who spends time with him, who admires him. A boy needs a man he can look up to. What he doesn't need is a shrink." (Christopher N. Bacorn, *Newsweek,* 7 December 1992, p. 13.) This need is not exclusive to boys, however. What can be concluded from the abundance of data, headlines, and cries for help? As David Blankenhorn concluded: "In short, the key is for men to be fathers. The key is for children to have fathers. The key is for society to create fathers. For society, the primary results of fatherhood are right-doing males and better outcomes for children." (*Fatherless America,* p. 26.) It is obvious what we must conclude: fathers matter.

This conclusion shouldn't be making headlines. In earlier times, fatherhood was known as patriarchy and was considered the *esse* of Hebrew psychology (see John B. Taylor, *Ezekiel: An Introduction and Commentary* [Downer Grove, Ill.: Inter-Varsity Press, 1969], p. 148). Patriarchy did not diminish matriarchy, nor did it decrease the importance of marriage or family. Patriarchy was, at one time, at the center of the family—not lingering in the periphery. Not only was it at the center, it was considered a noble role. The Hebrews even considered it sacred. We live in a world where the sacred is peripheral at best. It is considered corny by some and hypothetical by others, and many people do not even consider it as an option. Yet Elder James E. Faust has urged us to consider the roles of parenthood as sacred. He said: "In my opinion, members of the Church have the most effective cure for our decaying family life. It is for men, women, and children to honor and respect the divine roles of both fathers and mothers in the home." (In Conference Report, April 1993, p. 47.) The time has come to put the divine back into the role of fatherhood.

The Divine Father

If we take the position that respecting the divine role of fathers and mothers is the cure for our ailing society, we need to focus upon the divine role of fathers. Rather than considering all the preconceived notions of fatherhood from the media, tradition, culture, and the experts of human relationships and affairs, we should consider the role of divine fatherhood from a divine perspective. According to President Howard W. Hunter: "A man who holds the priesthood regards the family as ordained of God. Your leadership of the family is your most important and sacred responsibility. The family is the most important unit in time and in eternity and, as such, transcends every other interest in life." (In Conference Report, October 1994, p. 68.) The divine role of fatherhood is directly tied to the priesthood and to the nature and character of a priest.

The Priesthood Father

In ancient Israel, the high priest entered the Holy of Holies once a year on the day of Atonement. Like temple worship today, ancient temple worship was highly symbolic. The Holy of Holies, the most sacred place in the ancient temple, was symbolic of celestial glory. The dress of the high priest was quite elaborate; it included a breastplate, an ephod, a robe, a broidered coat, a mitre, and a holy girdle (see Exodus 28:4). The ephod was made of gold, blue, purple, and scarlet fine-twined linen with two shoulder pieces joined at the edges. Upon the ephod were two onyx stones where the names of the children of Israel were engraved six on each stone and set in gold. The weight of the ephod was borne upon the priest's shoulders. (See Exodus 28:5–12.)

The breastplate, like the ephod, was made of gold, blue, purple, and scarlet fine-twined linen. The breastplate, however, contained twelve jewels rather than two. Each of the stones was engraven with the name of one of the twelve tribes of Israel. Thus the names of the tribes of Israel were borne upon the heart of the High Priest. Dressed in the holy robes, the high priest would then enter the Holy of Holies, bearing the children of Israel upon his shoulders and on his heart. This symbolic act is not too far distant from the nature or character of the priesthood bearer today.

Modern priesthood holders bear the same responsibility as the ancient priests. Therefore, it is the responsibility of today's priesthood holder to bear his children upon his shoulders and on his heart. It is not enough to bear their weight temporally; the priesthood bearer must strive to bring his family into celestial glory, where families live in godly conditions. President Ezra Taft Benson reminded us that "fatherhood is not a matter of station or wealth; it is a matter of desire, diligence, and determination to see one's family exalted in the celestial kingdom. If that prize is lost, nothing else really matters." (In Conference Report, April 1981, p. 49.) With this sacred view of fatherhood in mind, President Harold B. Lee's statement that "the most important of the Lord's work you and I will ever do will be within the walls of our own homes" typifies the father's role and responsibility (*Stand Ye in Holy Places* [Salt Lake City: Deseret Book Co., 1974], p. 255). The most divine Father, God Himself, exemplifies this same mission. From a godly perspective, fatherhood is not only His work but His glory (see Moses 1:39).

Under the grand concept of the priesthood father, there is still hope for all fathers, even to those without power tools. A father's real responsibility is challenging and requires special effort. Brigham Young was once told to "take especial care of your family" (D&C 126:3). In light of the intense conditions of the day, when evil dares parade in open view without shame or fear, the divine role of a father is critical. Because of the significance of a father's role, it is of little wonder why President Benson has declared that "great things are required of fathers today" (in Conference Report, April 1981, p. 46).

3

Standards of Exaltation

Once fathers grasp their ultimate responsibility as dictated by their divine role, it is important to fully understand what the family must do to enter the celestial kingdom. As we talk about standards, it is important to understand *appropriate* standards, otherwise the discussion is limited. I have two primary concerns regarding standards, which can be shown in the following two examples.

As we prepared for Christmas one year, my youngest daughter excitedly told me that she had some Christmas money, and she described all of the wonderful gifts she planned to buy for her mother, brother, and sister. I couldn't help but feel excited as she beamed with enthusiasm. "Dad, will you go shopping with me?" Lauren asked as she opened her little hand, revealing four pennies. Her desire was genuine, her motives were pure, and her enthusiasm was irresistible; only her understanding of the price required for her desired goal was lacking. I am concerned that many Latter-day Saints understand the general goal and, like Lauren, truly desire the reward—but they have only a limited understanding of the expected price, or of the relationship between actions and eternal consequences.

The second example involves knowing the proper standards but choosing to live by a lower standard. My son and his friends spend hours playing basketball. We have an adjustable basketball standard, and the boys prefer to play with the hoop low enough for them to dunk. I guess that makes them feel like the big boys. I must admit there are moments when they actually play like the big boys—only on a smaller standard. While my son might rejoice in his accomplishments in driveway ball and feel that his game is at its peak, it is notably different from the *real* game and the official ten-foot standard. This became apparent as the youth league basketball season started. My son and his friends found a substantial difference between the normal ten-foot standards and the lower dunking standard with which they had fine-tuned their game. It definitely affected their play. Unlike Lauren with her pennies, Zachary had an understanding of how the game worked. As a matter of fact, he was quite good at playing the game—at a lower height. My concern is that many fathers understand the gospel and generally live the principles, but they become comfortable living the gospel standard as they choose. Unfortunately, the standards of gospel living they set for themselves and their families are not in harmony with the proper height. The transition to the proper standard is awkward and disheartening, and it requires more practice.

As we speak of fatherhood, it is important to understand the proper standards. Some fathers fine-tune their role according to a standard that is less than desirable, while others strain to achieve ends that are not only exasperating but of little long-term worth. If the father's role is to bring those in his stewardship into the presence of God, it is critical for fathers to understand the standards of judgment. It would be painful to be short even by a few pennies to pay the price needed to gain admission to our ultimate goal. Some of us need to review the basic standards of gospel living, such as faith, repentance, baptism, the gift of the Holy Ghost, the Word of Wisdom, tithing, chastity, offerings, and Sabbath worship—and some need to understand the full gospel standards more completely.

In June 1965 President David O. McKay impressed upon the members of the newly organized Church Building Committee that when our time in mortality is through, each of us will be required to answer certain questions. Fred Baker, a member of that committee, recorded these six questions or requests:

1. Give an accounting for your relationship with your spouse.
2. Give an accounting for your individual relationship with *each* of your children.
3. What have you personally done with the talents given you in the premortal existence?
4. How did you fulfill your stewardship in church assignments?
5. Were you honest in all your dealings?
6. What have you done to make a better city, state, and community?

I found these questions very enlightening and yet somehow completely different from what I expected. I had always imagined the Judgment to be something like a courtroom appearance, where a bench separated me from the judge. On the bench were mounds of evidence: Sunday School attendance rolls, sound bites of ill-spoken words or rumors passed along, broken panes of glass, evidence of broken promises, pictures of chalk outlines of all the insects killed for no reason, and a detailed record of my home teaching since Aaronic Priesthood days. Then there was the long line of witnesses waiting to testify either for me or against me. The questions described by President McKay, however, sound more like an interview than a trial. It is important to understand the probing nature of these questions, for they give an accurate standard for fathers to use in fulfilling their divine role. For example, every father will be asked to account for their individual relationship with *each* of their children. This question suggests a higher standard than does a question like "How are your children?" or, even more specifically, "How is Megan?" If we gauge our relationships according to general questions rather than the questions revealed by President McKay, we will be unable to properly answer the Lord's questions. What does it take for a father to give an accounting of his relationships with his family? First, it requires a relationship, and second, it requires the type of relationship that is significant to the Lord's standards.

Many fathers may be thinking at this point: *Everything is fine with my family relationships. We get along great . . . we're pals!* But the way we perceive and define our relationships with family members may be different from reality. A good measure of the accuracy of our perception of a relationship is to compare it with the perceptions of our family members. I had an eye-opening experience at a parent-teacher conference at the elementary school my son attended. My wife and I sat in the hall waiting for our turn to see our son's teacher. Artwork from my son's class was taped on the wall of the hall outside the classroom door. Naturally, I stood up and looked for my son's project. The conferences were held in March, so the theme was St. Patrick's Day. Students had answered the question, "If leprechauns really did exist, what would you wish for?" My son's wish was a "new car for my dad." At first I was moved that he would think of me. Then I read on. "My dad's car is broken, and he has to park on a hill every day when he goes to work so he can push it down the hill and get it started so he can come home." This fifth-grader's description was actually quite accurate. True, my alternator was broken, and I had to roll my car down the hill to jump-start it every day, but all this took place where very few people would see. It was private. Now every parent at parent-teacher conference knew my automobile woes in vivid detail. He had even drawn a picture of me pushing my car down a hill. Ouch! My wife just laughed.

My only consolation was reading the other students' papers. I was surprised at how many of the wishes had something to do with the students' fathers. I was startled to see one picture depicting an airplane on fire and headed toward certain doom. The explanation was simple and gripping: "I wish Delta Airlines would go out of business. Then my dad would be home more often." A bit dramatic, perhaps, but I believe it was heartfelt nonetheless. Picture after picture showed fathers playing catch, eating dinner with the family, or just smiling.

As adults, we have a tendency to explain away our actions. We carefully explain why we behave as we do as if our explanation makes it right. We tell our children that we really haven't been gone *all* that much or that grumpiness, getting mad, or being stern is all part of being a grown-up. "After all," we explain, "somebody has to make a living." I am fully aware of the demands on the time of family providers. It is difficult, frustrating, and draining to make ends meet, let alone nurture family relationships. Despite our explanations, however, reality is in the mind and heart of the beholder. A child's perceptions, excuses, and rationales can be just as valid as ours.

If we are to be accountable for our relationship with each member of our family, it is hard to imagine reporting at the Judgment that "they're fine, doing great." We need to make accurate assessments of our relationships in our divine fatherly role. So where do we start? One of the best methods of building relationships and checking the effectiveness of relationships while guiding and directing family members to the celestial kingdom is honest conversation.

Honest conversation can be awkward. "Son," you may say after audibly clearing your throat, "let's talk." I can't think of anything that drowns the fire of desire to talk more quickly than an announcement of "let's talk." I believe that many fathers *want* to talk with their children. I believe that they are *willing* to spend the necessary time to establish a relationship with their children. Yet the greatest inhibitor to this desire is that they aren't quite sure of what to do or how to do it—or they think it is probably too late to start. The next chapter should help you overcome those concerns.

4

Father's Interviews

According to a family organization survey, 78 percent of the parents interviewed stated that "the single most important factor for the success of the American family in the '90s is communication" (Carma Wadley, "National Family Week: Family Works," *Deseret News,* p. C1). While parents extolled the importance of communication, "only 35 percent of the children participating in the survey indicated that their families often 'sit and talk together'" (ibid.). Obviously, there is a gap between theory and practice. This is alarming because it demonstrates that while parents believe that communication is vital in families, not much is being done about it in the home.

Elder Horacio A. Tenorio counseled fathers to stand as "watchtowers" in protecting their families. With the ill winds of society beating upon family unity, we must stand ever vigilant in protecting our loved ones. Elder Tenorio suggested that "one of the watchtowers on our fortress can be the regular habit of a father's interview with each member of his family. Personal interviews are an important resource in maintaining the integrity of our fortress. Through them we become better acquainted with our children, learn about their problems and concerns, and establish open communication and trust that will enable us to foresee any danger, help them make decisions, and support them during difficult times." (In Conference Report, October 1994, pp. 29–30.) It is hard to think of any better way to protect family relationships from the brewing storms on the horizon than through such interviews.

I am sure that we have all had varied experiences with interviews, whether for a job, temple recommend, or performance evaluation. I remember my first job interview. I was an excited fifteen-year-old. Under the excitement, however, I had a taut stomach and a subtle dizziness. I would hope that a father's interview would be different from such an experience. Some interviews can be a time of celebration, while others are soul-searching reviews. A father's interview shouldn't be a dreadful experience but an anticipated regular event.

Elder N. Eldon Tanner suggested a sure foundation for successful interviews: "Let us always remember that our main purpose, assignment, and responsibility is to save souls. It is important that those we interview realize that they are *spirit children of God* and that *we love them,* and *let them know that we love them* and are interested in their welfare and in helping them succeed in life." (In Conference Report, October 1978, p. 59; emphasis in original.) The purpose of an interview, according to Elder Tanner is to "save souls." Therefore, a father's interview is more than just a checklist of behavioral items. It should be a time for growth, understanding, and acceptance. This is a unique experience for both father and children. A father's interview is more than just chatting or spending quality time with your children. This is not a job interview—they are already part of the company (and may even use your interview as a chance to get a raise!).

The Lord warned Joseph Smith in Doctrine and Covenants 68:25: "Inasmuch as parents have children in Zion . . . that teach them not to understand the doctrine of repentance, faith in Christ the Son of the living God, and of baptism, and the gift of the Holy Ghost by the laying on of the hands . . . the sin be upon the heads of the parents." Jacob emphasized this very point as he and his younger brother Joseph worked diligently to "magnify" their office as "teachers of this people" (Jacob 1:18–19). Both Jacob and Joseph interpreted magnification as teaching "the word of God with all diligence" (Jacob 1:19). The father's interview should be a sacred time of not only developing relationships but of paternal teaching. This is not to say that it is not important to have fun. The father's interview is not designed to take the place of family fun or individual time; it is an augmentation of our sacred role to teach in a setting that is conducive to the task.

The greatest difficulty of the paternal interview is deciding not whether it is important enough to do but how one should begin and go about the interview itself. Since the motive of the interview should be to save souls, an emphasis on teaching our family members is imperative. It should be mentioned, however, that what works well for some may not work well for others. My suggestions, therefore, are merely that—suggestions. The importance should be placed not on methods but on principles and purpose, which do not go out of style for those who endure.

Nuts and Bolts

Father's interviews should be regular. Elder Tenorio's suggestion that a father's interview be a regular habit is essential. The definition of *regular,* however, becomes tricky. Families are constantly changing, and each stage of family development is different. Therefore, the needs of the family must be considered when defining *regular*. In general, once a month seems to be a good rule of thumb for keeping abreast of changes and needs in the family. Another good rule of thumb is to set a specific day for interviews so that both father and family member not only remember when the interview should be held but can anticipate it as well. There is power in knowing that each month, at an arranged time, there will be a chance to discuss things that matter, receive counsel, or just be reminded that each individual matters. For me, interviews work best every fast Sunday. Setting a regular day promotes a constant pattern and makes it easy to remember. Obviously, flexibility is an important issue, but consistency is tantamount.

Father's interviews should be held in a suitable place. Each interview should be private and in a setting that invites rather than hampers comfort. It really doesn't matter where the interview takes place (office, living room, den) as long as both you and your children feel comfortable and the setting contributes to the fulfillment of the interview's intended purpose. My personal favorite setting is our family hammock in the summertime. It is relaxing and a nice change of pace.

Father's interviews should begin and end with prayer. As with all things of importance, inspiration should be sought during father's interviews. Elder Tenorio felt that "a loving interview guided by the Spirit can give direction to our children's lives, bring about necessary adjustments or changes, and may even result in miracles" (in Conference Report, October 1994, p. 30). The scriptures offer example after example of the importance of being led by the Spirit. Entering darkened Jerusalem to obtain the plates of brass, Nephi was led by the Spirit, not knowing beforehand what he should do (see 1 Nephi 4:6). There is no better source of light for guiding difficult or seemingly impossible situations as the inspiration of God. I believe that great power comes to a family that not only prays together but shares inspiration's power and guidance *between* family members as well. Since this interview begins with prayer, it is also appropriate to end with prayer. Allowing both father and family member to pray is important; it allows the Spirit to permeate both parties.

A father should interview each family member individually. Since each father will be asked, as President McKay suggested, about their relationship with each of their children, every family member should have the opportunity to have a private father's interview. A father's interview should be designed to meet the needs of the individual. An interview held with a seventeen-year-old is different from an interview with a two-year-old. Likewise, it is just as important to spend twenty minutes alone with a fifth-grader as with an infant. I realize that infants do not talk and that three-year-olds have a very short attention span, but we can still find effective ways to "interview" them.

As fathers spend individual time with their children in a monthly interview, they establish tradition and build trust in the early years. Fathers get to know their children, and children get to know their fathers. More important, children with a foundation of personal interviews know that they are cared for and loved and that they have open access to help, should the need arise. Elder A. Theodore Tuttle suggested: "Fathers, draw close to your children. Learn to communicate. Learn to listen. This means giving a father's most valuable commodity—time! Only good results occur when a father interviews his sons and daughters regularly. He can know their problems and their hopes. He can align himself with them as their unconditional friend. To the extent we become friends with our children in unconditional love, to that extent we become like our Heavenly Father." (In Conference Report, October 1973, p. 87.)

I would encourage you to talk to your infants, pray for them, sing songs with your two- and three-year-olds, and counsel with your teens. A father's interview should take as long (or as short) as needed. The length of the interview should meet the needs of your children. Often, my younger children let *me* know when the interview is over. Filling time is not the goal of the interview—communicating is. I fear that some fathers may feel it is too late to start interviewing their children because their children have already moved on or just plain moved out. But here is an interesting question: When do you grow out of your role as a father?

I remember venting to my father one day (venting is an exercise that lies somewhere between murmuring and throwing a tantrum) about how difficult life was. I was finishing graduate school, worried about housing, and barely making ends meet. As I outlined trials, events, and circumstances that I thought would have surely given even Job difficulty, I couldn't help but notice my father's deliberate exercise of patience. There were times when I felt he was trying not to laugh. I remember saying something about how it gets easier when you get older and about how you don't have to worry about things anymore once you hit a certain stage in your life. It was around this point that my father laughed out loud. His laugh caused a twinge of anxiety in my mind that maybe life would always have its challenges, worries, and adventures.

My father then gave me good counsel, reassured me about the future, and gave me a father's blessing. Through our conversation, I realized that my father would always be my father. He still worried and prayed for me—even though I had long since moved out of his house and started a family of my own. I have realized that my father still plays a significant role in my adult life. I need his counsel, perspective, and example. Fatherhood does not have an expiration date. You will not find a bar code and a "best if used before" date stamped under the scalp of every father. Regardless of age, a father's accountability for his children is vital; therefore regular interviews are critical.

A father's interview should gather essential information. One of the difficulties of interviewing is listening. Listening is different from waiting for your turn to talk. By the same token, listening and never talking isn't effective either. In order to achieve a balance in interviews, it is helpful to follow a guideline—or template, if you will. I don't recommend a checklist of questions but prefer a format that helps an interview be concise while still making a fairly good assessment of the situation. Remember, this is only a suggestion that has worked out well for others. The hows are not quite as important as the whys.

The template I have found most helpful was developed after considerable fussing. When I realized that I should be interviewing my children on a regular basis, I thought about what I wanted to find out. I sat for long hours contemplating what I wished my father had known about me at different times of my life, or things he didn't know but should have known. After considerable thought, I decided that my interviews would need to build relationships, give me a keener understanding of my children's activities, help me determine their balance in life, help me learn of their future plans, strengthen family relationships, and help me handle family management issues. I also wanted a time when we could have a forum experience for discussions about matters that I or my children felt were important. At first, I thought this type of interview would take about a week. However, after I had a clear picture of what I wanted to accomplish, I developed a concise form to help me accomplish my desired goal. The form I use is one that works well *for me*. It fits in my planner in a section titled "Family Inventory." My form is small and somewhat difficult to write on, but once again it fits my needs.

During the interview, I take notes on the form. There is no need to feel guilty about writing things down during your interviews; in fact, I recommend you explain why you're taking

Family Inventory

Name **Megan**   Date **April 2, 1996**

Intellectual (Education)	Physical (Activities)
School-very fine. Working on fractions. Miss Sykes a "very great teacher."	Dance-great. Sometimes doesn't like dance-having to do stretch-splits. Plans to play T-ball.
Goal: Color in free time.	Goal: Be well rounded.
Social (Friends)	Spiritual (Church)
Best friend-Shabrom-is kind. Steven B. pinches (he sits diagonal from Meg).	Going fine. Teacher is "really great." Jesus is still living. Saying her prayers every night.
Goal: Be patient!	Goal: Sometimes say prayers on her own.
Career	Dreams and Wishes
Saw a film on nurses. Great movie! She has been thinking of being a nurse since she was 6.	Having a "packed" Toys R Us. Having a major diamond.
Goal: Read about nurses. Get good high school and college grades	Goal: Go to celestial kingdom

FEEDBACK FOR FAMILY

Dad	Mom	Zach	Megan
Quit: Going to work	Quit: Taking away privileges	Quit: Teasing	Quit:
Keep: Giving hugs, kisses; playing	Keep: Hugs, kisses; playing a lot	Keep: Sharing; hugs, kisses	Keep: Hugs
Start: Playing more!	Start:	Start: Getting along better	Start:
Lauren			
Quit: Losing temper	Quit:	Quit:	Quit:
Keep: Sharing; hugs, kisses	Keep:	Keep:	Keep:
Start:	Start:	Start:	Start:

Concerns, Suggestions, Challenges

Get along. Talk about problems. No tattling. Temper tantrums, stay in control, reminders. Mind when Zach baby-sits. Doing a great job at school!

Family Inventory

Name_____ Date _____

Intellectual (Education)	Physical (Activities)
_____	_____
_____	_____
_____	_____
Goal:	Goal:
Social (Friends)	**Spiritual (Church)**
_____	_____
_____	_____
_____	_____
Goal:	Goal:
Career	**Dreams and Wishes**
_____	_____
_____	_____
_____	_____
Goal:	Goal:

FEEDBACK FOR FAMILY

Quit:	Quit:	Quit:	Quit:
Keep:	Keep:	Keep:	Keep:
Start:	Start:	Start:	Start:
Quit:	Quit:	Quit:	Quit:
Keep:	Keep:	Keep:	Keep:
Start:	Start:	Start:	Start:

Concerns, Suggestions, Challenges

notes. Taking notes helps me remember our conversation during the month. Prior to meeting the next month, I review my notes from the previous interview and jot a few things down for follow-through. Perhaps the best reason for keeping notes is my hope that when each of my children leave our home to start their own home, I will copy their interview sheets and bind them as a booklet and present this record of their life's progression as a gift. What a wonderful legacy of their growing years! I will also keep a copy for myself. Think of the memories! As I previously mentioned, it is important to continue your interviewing stewardship even after family vacancies occur. Perhaps your form can be altered for older or married children, and perhaps interviews can be completed by telephone, mail, E-mail, or fax. Although adjustments to method may occur, family assessment should continue.

The form I have included here is an example of an interview form from a previous interview with my daughter Megan. (She gave me permission to publish this.) A blank form is also included, and each section is explained below.

A Balanced Inventory

It is important that as stewards we foster and nurture well-balanced development in our children. Instead of talking only about sports, hobbies, or other interests that naturally come up, it is important that we discuss all areas of life. Perhaps the greatest reason I feel strongly about a holistic approach is illustrated by an experience I had long ago while studying the New Testament. Christ admonished us to be as both he and our Father in Heaven are (see Matthew 5:48; 3 Nephi 12:48). As I thought about becoming like Christ, I wondered about his development as a youth. There really isn't much written in the scriptures about the youthful years of the Savior's life. There are, however, bits and pieces left as appetizers for those searching to know him. One of my favorites is found in the book of Luke. Small in size but encompassing in depth, this fourteen-word reference provides enough material for years of contemplation: "And Jesus increased in wisdom and stature, and in favour with God and man" (Luke 2:52). This compact verse, which provides a wonderful understanding of Jesus Christ and gives an appropriate model for those who desire to be more like him, seems like a good standard of development: to increase "in wisdom and stature, and in favour with God and man." In other words, this tremendous verse includes four areas of mortal development: intellectual, physical, spiritual, and social. These areas of development became the basis for my family inventory sheet. Thus, the first section of my interview discussion concerns these four areas of my children's lives: intellectual (education), physical (activities), social (friends), and spiritual (church).

Intellectual (education). It is here that I find out what my children's interests are intellectually. They explain what they are learning in school, their frustrations and successes, and how they feel about their teachers. I have found that my best role during this part of the interview is to elicit a response by asking something such as "Tell me about your teacher, Miss Burton." Then I listen. After that, "Why?" seems to be my most preferred question. I'm not sure, but I wonder if that is a slight payback for all those years where my children bombarded me with "Why this?" or "Why that?" or "Why why?" Now it is my turn to ask why!

I ask what types of books they are reading (or if they are reading at all), or sometimes I quiz them on general facts about geography, history, or trivia. Some of my fondest memories as a father are the times I have heard my children express their appreciation and admiration for a good teacher, book, or historical figure or just their excitement for a new subject. It is during this time that I have sung the alphabet song, counted to one hundred, or practiced naming colors with my younger children. I have explained a little pre-algebra or *tried* to explain why it was important to learn about geometry to my older children. I am astounded by the things my children are learning (or at least exposed to) at their age. I marvel at the opportunities my children are having, and I feel encouraged about their possibilities. I too have learned new things. For example, I have found that my literacy in geography is antiquated (after all the political changes in the past fifteen years)—but luckily my youngest children can help me.

Physical (activities). This area of development is easy to discuss for most fathers. It includes sports, dancing, and physical development. I love to hear my children describe their victories and concerns. My favorite part is to hear them tell about a game from their vantage point. What excitement, thrill, and agony! I ask about their reasons for playing games and about coaches, and I point out the importance of developing our bodies and taking good care of ourselves. We talk about personal hygiene, eating issues, exercise, and other physical concerns. It is a good time to put physical activities such as sports into proper perspective.

Social (friends). This area has become increasingly important in my interviews. It is during this part that I learn who my children's friends are. I ask who they consider their best friends to be and why, and I write down each name as it is revealed. It has been fun to see the changes in friends over the years. This is also a good time to review dating experiences and appropriate social activities.

Spiritual (church). While all areas are important for complete development, this is my favorite section. In my estimation, meaning and depth are natural parts of this area. It is here where I hear about my children's budding testimonies, questions, and even doubts. They describe their Primary and Sunday School teachers in ways that I have never considered. I ask them what they are learning during their Sunday instruction, remind them about their prayers, and try to answer any gospel questions they might have. Best of all, I have the opportunity to listen to my children's testimonies as well as bear my testimony to them.

Career. Each month my children tell me what they want to do when they grow up. It is important to allow your children to express their desires and not just reaffirm your expectations. Although it is difficult to distance yourself from the career decisions of your children, this part of the interview should be free of bias, especially with younger children. There are times, however, when a little supervision is important. For example, for months one of my daughters would answer my question, "What do you want to be when you grow up?" by saying matter-of-factly, "A monkey." While this probably would have been a typical answer during one of Tarzan's interviews, it just didn't fit our part of the jungle. At times like these, parental perspective becomes a necessary interjection. There is, of course, a monumental difference between wanting to become a monkey and wanting to become a doctor, lawyer, teacher, artist, or construction worker—yet some parents respond to some professions as if their child had said "monkey." While we want the best for our children and can often offer them mature guidance and suggestions, we also must allow them their agency.

In order to exercise agency, one must have an understanding of choices and consequences. You really wouldn't be much of a teacher during an interview if you only jotted down the information and then quickly moved on to the next subject. It is important to discuss what must be done in order to accomplish the child's desired career goal. For example, if your child states that he or she wants to become a professional athlete (a popular desire for many young men), rather than reacting by telling them that their desire is unrealistic or impractical, teach them what is required to become a professional athlete. Outline the necessary skills, physical demands, and knowledge required to compete at that level of the game. Tell them about the hours of practice, possible injuries, and politics as well as the thrill of a cheering crowd and the fun of playing the game. This exercise is not to convict or convince—rather it is an exercise in teaching by making relevant information available. Children should understand that most athletes have some college education and that they must be successful in their sport, pass physicals, and then be *chosen* to play. Let unbiased information be the convincing factor or the dissuading argument for any profession. If you only present the cons and not the pros, your presentation will seem stifling and your child's trust could be weakened.

Dreams and wishes. This part of the interview allows a glimpse of your child's personality. Sometimes I'll ask: "If you had three wishes, what would you wish for?" or "What would you do with a million dollars?" or "If you could have anything, what would it be?" Such questions allow the imagination to work, the inner desires to flow, and the private person to speak. This allows me to know more about my children beyond the basic facts and figures.

Another advantage of asking about dreams and wishes comes from unexpected lessons. For example, part of my son's wish list included a tree house. He was consistent in his requests, never wavering. After many interviews, I suggested that he first wish for a tree, because we don't have a tree on our property large enough for a tree house. It was as if a light suddenly went on in his mind, and we started laughing. It dawned on me that he was wondering, after all these months, why I was opposed to having a tree house. After this experience, he understood *why* we didn't have a tree house—at least, not yet. He got the message that I would have liked him to have a tree house (we even started drawing up plans together) but that the logistics of his dream were just a little off. For the next couple of interviews, I found it interesting that on the top of his wish list was a tree!

I have found asking about dreams not only beneficial but also fun—even with my wife. We often ask each other what he or she might request from a genie. Most couples share their dreams and wishes in the early stages of their courtship and marriage, but unfortunately our dreams become invaded with commonplace realities. When "walking barefoot on a warm beach" is replaced with "you taking the garbage out" as one of the three wishes, something is wrong. There is magic in dreaming and hope. President Spencer W. Kimball once quoted the architect Daniel H. Burnham, who said, "Make no little plans, they have no magic to stir men's blood" ("The Gospel Vision of the Arts," *Ensign,* July 1977, p. 5). When we catch a glimpse of someone's dreams, I believe we see, just for a quick moment, deep inside them. Perhaps it is a glimpse of their hopeful soul.

Goals. I have included on my family inventory form a box for goals in each of the sections mentioned above. It is often helpful to set a goal to work on in some of the areas during the month. Keep in mind your objectives, however. If your interviews are just another way of making children feel that they are not measuring up, the role of steward is shifted to that of judge.

Feedback. Many years ago I attended a class where I was deeply impacted by some of the instructor's comments. I fussed a great deal over Tom DeLong's suggestions about balancing career, family, and personal identity. He talked about a management technique called "QKS" that establishes feedback systems. It is based on three questions: "What should I *quit* doing?" "What should I *keep* doing?" and finally "What should I *start* doing?" I could see the importance of establishing feedback in my family and I thought this formula would be beneficial, so I included it on my interview form.

Ask your children, "What am I doing as your father that you wish I would *quit* doing?" There is a certain amount of bravery required to ask such a question. You may find out that you are human, or, worse yet, you may discover that your *family* has found out how human you really are! Be careful that once you hear the feedback you requested you don't immediately start explaining, justifying, or defending yourself. Listen carefully, ask questions so that you fully understand, and then write their comments down.

Next, ask, "What am I as your father doing that you hope I will *keep* doing?" I always clinch my teeth and feel my insides get tight, because for me this question can be just as painful as the preceding question. I just hope they can think of *one* thing. I fear hearing, "Gee, Dad, I can't really think of anything right now. Let's come back to that one later." I have even considered making a list of my admirable fatherly traits and asking them to choose one they like. While this method may prove less painful, it somehow misses the mark. I must admit, however, that some of my best unexpected kudos for being a father have come when my children have answered this question.

Finally, ask, "What would you like me as your father to *start* doing?" Now is when I hope they can't think of anything to say! I should forewarn you, however, to brace yourself for some interesting responses. They range anywhere from "Don't go to work anymore" to "Buy a new car."

Follow this same line of questioning about each member of the family. For example, you might ask, "What do you hope that your sister, Lauren, will keep doing?" This has been a great help to build stronger family unity. During the course of interviews, I usually share (unless asked to keep it confidential) each child's concerns with the other children: "Did you know that your sister loves it when you help her with homework?" "It is hard on some of your siblings when you lose your temper; did you know that?"

Naturally, all of this information becomes an important part of conversations between my wife and me. We sometimes discover that the way we see a problem is not the way our children see it.

Concerns, suggestions, and challenges. This section is reserved for areas of concern I might have and for items my children might be worrying about. Sometimes we have plenty to talk about in these areas, and other times we just touch base. We have discussed manners, values, relationships, appropriate entertainment, household management issues, and morality. During the month I might jot down a few concerns that I think of or observe in preparation for the upcoming interviews. I have had the opportunity to talk about commandments, sexuality, health concerns, and even politics. This is a natural forum that, if handled well, nurtures discussion on any topic. It is important to remember that all is fair and open to discussion.

5

Interviewing: Behind the Scenes

Although the interview is a good means to an end, it is important to keep the interview from becoming the end in itself. If an agenda becomes the most important part of interviewing, the purpose and benefit are lost. I can remember several personal interviews that were similar in format but completely different in feel, outcome, and what they instilled inside me. For example, I have had numerous temple recommend interviews, all very similar in format and content. Yet I can remember one interview that stands out because of the unusual way I felt from the moment I walked into the office to the final handshake. From the beginning, I felt the interest of my ecclesiastical leader. Everything about the interview was an *invitation.* As we talked about temple worthiness, I often felt prompted to say more than yes. He asked follow-up questions, expressed appreciation for my worthiness, and voiced general concerns he had for the stake. His reflective manner invited *me* to reflect. I guess what made this experience singular was that during this interview I felt as if I were his only appointment for that night. It seemed as if the most important person in that office was me. Like most interviews, this interview was genuine, followed the specific format, and was not necessarily lengthy. This time, however, it was different: I felt as if I was interviewed with *meaning*.

Because of this experience, I feel it is important to mention some suggestions that will help *behind the scenes* of effective interviews. I feel uncomfortable calling these suggestions *techniques,* because that sounds too automated. These principles are important because they are principles which invite. Without understanding the necessary background behind the scenes of an effective father's interview, one's interviews will be just like all the other interviews in the world. Before your next interview, it may be helpful to thoughtfully review the following six considerations.

1. *Seek to understand the meaning that events, things, and experiences have for others.* As you interview, topics that don't necessarily interest you personally or strike the same emotional chord in you as they do in your children will inevitably arise. If, however, you fail to understand the *meaning* behind the event, thing, or statement, you will appear uninterested and uncaring. Children usually respond to this posture with exasperated gasps, rolling their eyes and shaking their heads as they say, "You *just* don't understand."

This principle is obviously not restricted to children, for it is a key in marriage as well as in any other relationship. Remember, it isn't the *thing* itself that signals importance, it is the *meaning* behind the object. For example, I remember reading about a father who received a clip-on dinosaur for Christmas from his five-year-old son. Not sure what to do with this gift, he clipped the dinosaur to his lapel. Immediately, he saw the excitement in his son's eyes as the boy's father proudly wore his gift. I identified with this story immediately, as do many parents. We have piles of gadgets made out of Popsicle sticks, string, macaroni, yarn, old cans, and clay. Unfortunately, too many fathers praise the homemade or hand-picked gift only to place it quickly back into the box and shelve it with all the gifts of years past. "No, Daddy," they say, "you're suppose to *wear* it!" Bless their honest and naive hearts, they really thought you were putting it away because you *didn't know* you were supposed to wear it. Ha! Understanding the meaning behind the craft, however, is where bonds are forged and the power of communication is made whole. Our clip-on dinosaur dad concluded: "So the next time you see an adult wearing a crude paper tie or a 'cool' five-cent (removable) caterpillar tattoo, don't bother feeling sorry for him. If you tell him he looks silly, he'll say, 'Maybe, but I've got a five-year-old son who thinks I'm the best thing since peanut butter, and there isn't enough money in the U.S. Treasury to make me take it off.'" (Dan Schaeffer, "Why I Wear a Plastic Dinosaur," *Reader's Digest,* June 1994, p. 126.)

Thank goodness for refrigerators, the established showcase of notable objects. While this type of refrigerator is never found on the pages of *House Beautiful,* this museum of meaning is one of the most beautiful decorations of the heart. The fridge becomes the centerpiece of the home not for what is inside it but for what is on it—usually taped in layers. Children take pride when their work makes it onto the fridge hall of fame. It is almost as if they know their work has been validated if it makes it on the fridge. I have even considered placing some of my things—papers from work, pictures—on our fridge. As we learn to pick up clues, locations, and phrases that signal significant meaning in the lives of our family members and as we begin to realize the meaning behind *things,* they become more meaningful to us too.

Not long ago, I gave a presentation in which I thought an object might illustrate a point I wanted to make. My assigned topic was honor. I used Bishop Robert D. Hales's conference address concerning his military experience and motto of "return with honor" as the foundation of my address (see Conference Report, April 1990, pp. 51–55). I remember my father telling stories similar to Elder Hales's from his own military experiences in the air force during World War II. I called my father and asked if I might borrow his flight wings from the war as an object to illustrate honor. He willingly obliged. I told him that I would pick the wings up on my way to the airport. Instead, my father offered to drive me to the airport to catch my flight. As we were driving, my father took his wings out of his pocket. He told me that he had polished the sterling silver wings as he got them ready for me. "You didn't have to do that, Dad," I quickly responded. As he handed me his wings, he began to weep. Then I realized that he almost *had* to polish those wings. There was meaning behind them. Those wings represented an important part of my father: commitment, value, patriotism, loss of life and friends, honor, and his willingness to entrust them to me. When I pinned those wings on my suit coat before my presentation, I was really pinning on all the things those wings stood for. My father's meaning was transferred to me. Through a pair of shiny silver wings, I felt cloaked in love for my father and his honor. I cherish those wings today. That piece of sterling silver has become meaningful and filled with legacy for me too.

So the next time you hear about a failed test, botched date, lost job, or how somebody named Rob didn't say hi today, it might not be the end of the world to you, but it might be for a sixteen-year-old. As we understand the background and emotions of events, things, and memories, we understand their meaning. Rather than telling our children to forget about it, move on, or grow up, we can address the deeper meaning rather than the surface appearance and build perspective.

2. *Be aware of agendas.* Although you may make time to hold interviews, your manner can communicate a different

agenda than you intended. A distinct aura of "Let's get this over with" is difficult to hide. Take into account the age of your children, their situations, and your time limitations as well as theirs. Remember that the agenda of a five-year-old is different from yours. Once while I was interviewing one of my daughters we were discussing her physical activities, specifically her dance class. She wanted to show me what she had learned. I was tired from a long fast Sunday (is that a contradiction in terms?), we were only on the first part of the form, and I knew I still had one more interview to go. Luckily for me, this daughter is filled with joy and was unrelenting. The next thing I knew, not only was she dancing around the room but she had me dancing *with* her. Every moment of that interview was forever etched in our relationship. Her agenda became my agenda—and I shudder to think that I almost missed it. Preschoolers are wiggily, preteens rarely look at you let alone in your general direction, and teens roll their eyes and communicate with muddled grunts. Nonetheless, we work together to accommodate growth.

3. *Teach your children what priesthood, marriage, and fatherhood are.* I remember getting a model car kit from a neighbor once when I was younger. *Why would anyone give away a model?* I wondered. The cellophane wrapping was already removed from the box, so I thought I should check the contents to see if anything was missing. Luckily, I found all the parts still intact and neatly arranged. From my observation, the only thing missing from the box was the set of instructions. I had assembled a number of models in my time, so I figured it couldn't be that hard to put it together on my own. After all, I thought, if you've built one model car, you've built them all! I spread all the parts of the car on a table and, with glue in hand, eagerly began my task. My completed model resembled a car— vaguely. However, it lacked the finished look of my other models. This was probably due to the fact that I still had a box full of

unused parts. An accurate set of instructions can make all the difference in the world—even to seemingly obvious tasks.

Many of life's participants are trying on their own to make mortality work. Without a set of instructions, a teacher, an example, or any other resources, they attempt to put their lives together. No wonder so many people feel that their life doesn't have that finished look or feel. An accurate set of instructions should come with each new stage in life, each newly assumed responsibility, each significant change. Unfortunately, instructions are very rarely passed on to those approaching a new threshold in life. I can't think of any situation better than a personal interview during which to instruct our children about weightier matters.

While Alma was interviewing his son Helaman, he gave him the plates and charged him to be the record keeper (see Alma 37). Alma sets a wonderful example of the *teaching* responsibility of a father to his son. On this important occasion, Helaman is obviously receiving a new mantle and responsibility. However, a more subtle, powerful message can be captured from the text. After giving some basic background about the plates, Alma *teaches* his son exactly what the records are. You might say, "They are the histories of his people, of course!" While you are right, such an explanation barely stirs the soul. Not willing to simply give away the records, Alma impresses upon his son's mind the value of the records he has just received. These records "bringeth about the salvation of many souls" (Alma 37:7) and would enlarge the memory of the people, convince the people of the errors of their ways, and bring them to a knowledge of their God (see Alma 37:8). Alma makes sure that Helaman understands that these records will be the "means of bringing many thousands . . . to the knowledge of their Redeemer" (Alma 37:10). I marvel at how Alma impresses upon Helaman the importance of being a faithful record keeper, but I love how he lets Helaman know what a great privilege it is to keep something as significant, meaningful, and vital as the message on the plates.

In like manner, fathers should teach their children how important it is to be baptized and receive the Holy Ghost. They should explain the importance of priesthood ordinations, father's blessings, and patriarchal blessings. But fathers must communicate *why* these events are so important. Imagine the power of a father sitting down with his son prior to his son's receiving the Aaronic Priesthood and explaining to him not only what is going to happen but why it is important. Somewhere during that conversation, the father will likely recount the blessings of the priesthood and what it means to be a priesthood holder. In another interview, a father might explain the importance of eternal marriage to a daughter who will shortly be married. "This is why it is so important," her father would say as he explains the significance of covenants and the sacred responsibilities of marriage. Like Alma with Helaman, there is a special power that comes in teaching the *meaning* and *purpose* of significant milestones. In father's interviews, rather than teaching just cursory facts we must teach meaning. We cannot afford to allow the world to teach our families what marriage is, how families function, and what we should hold sacred.

4. *Share.* In one of my favorite cartoon strips, a father, unable to sleep, laments to his wife: "It's funny. When I was a kid, I thought grown-ups never worried about anything. I trusted my parents to take care of everything, and it never occurred to me that they might not know how. I figured that once you grew up, you automatically knew what to do in any given scenario." Then comes the clincher. With a blank stare fixed upon his face, the father mutters: "I don't think I'd have been in such a hurry to reach adulthood if I'd known the whole thing was going to be ad-libbed." The phrase *ad-libbed adulthood* has a maddening yet hauntingly accurate tone.

For most children, there is an invisible barrier between parents and *real* people. While real people are struggling to make ends meet, overcoming personal weaknesses, and generally making mistakes along the way, parents never make mistakes, feel frustrated, or get dejected. They never have outlandish dreams or do things on a whim. Impulsive behavior? Not parents. When children find a touch of humanity in their parents, they are shocked to the core. "How could they?" they ask. "They are parents." It is usually beyond most youthful imaginations that parents could even be tempted. "Tempted?" most children would ask. "With what?" As I have wondered why this perception exists, I've concluded it is mostly the adults' or parents' fault. Most adults don't want to talk about it—life, I mean. Thus adulthood is shrouded in secrecy, and this attitude is passed from one generation to the next. It becomes a vicious cycle.

Adequate preparation, whether for adulthood, a mission, marriage, or parenthood, is achieved by looking to those who have trodden the paths of mortality before us. From their examples (both good and bad), we learn to chart our own direction. Keeping the rigors of life a secret is not only annoying to those embarking on the trip but also grossly unfair. Some may feel uncomfortable offering suggestions and advice. "Who am I to help?" they might question. "I'm still having a hard time figuring *my* life out!"

We must never forget the value personal experience can have in teaching those who have not yet walked the paths of life we have already ventured upon. Elder Jeffrey Holland talked of this special teaching role: "We who have already walked that portion of life's path that you are now on try to call back to you something of what we have learned. We shout encouragement. We try to warn of pitfalls or perils along the way. Where possible we try to walk with you and keep you close to our side. Believe it or not, we too were young once, though I know that strains the very limits of your imaginations. . . . But as the years have gone by we have learned many lessons beyond those of youth. . . . Why do you think we now try so hard and worry so much and want the very best for you? It is because we have been your age and you have never been ours, and we have learned some things you do not yet know." (In Conference Report, April 1995, p. 52.)

Too many adults are unwilling to offer words of warning, advice, or comfort to those who are beginning their journey on similar paths. This attitude cannot be right. I can't help but think of father Lehi in this context. After struggling to make his way to the tree of life, he eats of its fruit and is filled with "great joy" (1 Nephi 8:12). His first reaction is to find his family so they too might partake of the joy. At a distance, he notices Sariah, Sam, and Nephi and calls to them, for they stood "as if they knew not whither they should go" (v. 14). Heeding Lehi's beckoning voice, they come to the tree and eat of its harvest. It would have been a sad commentary had Lehi noticed his directionless family members and left them to fend for themselves, figure it out on their own, or just deal with it. I can't imagine Lehi shrugging his shoulders, turning his back on those walking the path, and exclaiming: "I had to figure it out for myself, so they can too." Those of us who know what it is like to be one of those who have "stood as if they knew not whither they should go" have long cherished a voice of warning, comfort, encouragement, and direction. We all have had sufficient personal experience (whether good or bad) to warn and encourage others in their journeys of mortality.

Another benefit of sharing life's lessons is that we build relationships as we share things about ourselves. Things of the self include people, experiences, memories, opinions, and thoughts that have claim upon our own hearts. Because of the sensitive nature of these experiences, most people usually tuck them away deep inside the heart. I have talked with hundreds of youth around the country. It intrigues me how many of them have no real sense of identifying with their parents. Most would squirm if they were asked questions about their parents on a test. I imagine this would be a category on the TV game show *Jeopardy* that would make even the most knowledgeable nervous. "I'll take 'My Parents' for two hundred, Alex." I know some individuals who don't know even the basics about those living in their household, such as birthdays, grades, activities, or church advancements. So how could they hope to answer the daily double when it comes to matters of the heart?

I find it interesting that as I talk with teenagers around the country only a handful can tell me the basics about their parents. The majority cannot tell me their parents' birthdays, how they met, where they were married, what they do for a living, or their favorite color and food. It is incredible. We have a generation of people who live in the same house for an extended period of time who know very little about each other. It is almost as if we live with strangers. As I have helped prospective missionaries prepare their applications many can't answer the question on the form that asks for the nationality of their ancestors. Many of my missionaries have no idea of their family heritage. I find this lack of general awareness disconcerting, but what I find alarming is a corollary: If a child does not share in the general factual details of their parents' lives (and vice versa), they more than likely do not share deeper, more meaningful things with their parents.

I remember the first time my father told me about the fears he had when he entered college. It nearly floored me. My father, scared? That conversation, however, not only helped me understand my father better but it validated me. I knew what it was like to be scared, although I rarely admitted it. It was refreshing to know that sometimes my parents were scared, had dreams, were tempted, and sometimes used poor judgment.

This doesn't condone poor judgment; it just let me know that I didn't hold a monopoly on it. Sharing personal experiences, fears, and frustrations allows relationships to be *real*. There are times when more than anything else—including advice—I needed someone who could just say, "I know what you mean."

5. *Be bold enough to ask and brave enough to keep quiet.* Some fathers perceive a father's interview as a time when the father talks and his children listen and occasionally answer "Yes, Dad" and "No, Dad." It is written that "to every thing there is a season, and a time to every purpose under the heaven" (Ecclesiastes 3:1). This is a good perspective to have during an interview. There is a time to ask questions and a time to listen carefully. As a matter of fact, verse seven from the same chapter reminds us that there is "a time to keep silence, and a time to speak." The secret seems to be achieving a balance between the two.

Rather than risk hearing about something they don't want to know about, many fathers just won't ask. Since the things fathers don't want to hear about are the very things children generally don't bring up in conversation with their parents, a widening gap is formed and little help is rendered. If you feel that your children will tell you when they are ready, you may be in for a long wait. It is the responsibility of the father to be bold enough to ask. Elder Carlos E. Asay told of a time when his wife was concerned whether one of their sons was truly decided about serving a mission. Elder Asay entered his son's room and sat on his bed. In what was probably a natural yet bold manner, Elder Asay asked, "Son, are you still planning on serving a mission?" "Yes," he answered. Then Elder Asay continued: "Son, do you know what qualifies a young man to serve a mission? Do you know what *worthiness* means?" Elder Asay awaited a reply. His son answered, "Yes, Dad. I understand the requirements and standards of worthiness that must be met." Up to this point, this father and son were laying a foundation. According to

Elder Asay, their conversation was straight to the point. As I imagine this father-to-son exchange, I don't see any lecturing, drawn-out analogies, or long-winded explanations. Obviously, they were not necessary at this time for this child. Elder Asay could have easily left his son's room and reported to his wife that their son was planning on a mission, and that would have been the end of the story. However, there was more to the story. I was already impressed, but my attitude turned to admiration as Elder Asay continued: "I have one last question: Are you clean and worthy to serve? Could you accept a call if one were issued you today?" His son replied: "It isn't easy. Temptation is real and found everywhere. However, since you've asked, I am clean and I am worthy to serve." Elder Asay described this experience as "wonderful, beautiful, spontaneous, and sanctifying." I wholeheartedly agree. He kissed his son, told him of his love, and bid him good night. I cannot help but ponder upon Elder Asay's son's reason for opening up: "Since you've asked . . ." I included this example because it demonstrates the boldness often required of fathers to ask the appropriate questions. (In Conference Report, October 1983, p. 18.)

Fathers must exhibit the courage to ask those questions that need to be asked. By the same token, the answers to these questions must be met with a deep sense of control. Fathers must be brave enough to keep quiet. For some reason, most of us have a tendency to jump right in and give advice. It is almost as if we have to hurry to get it in, otherwise it will be too late. Good advice is timely, which makes it enduring. Elder Marvin J. Ashton said, "Wise is the man who says what needs to be said, but not all that could be said" (in Conference Report, October 1976, p. 127). Patience in solving *someone else's* problems is a trait that builds confidence and trust in relationships. Unfortunately, most of us easily glide into an alter ego when we assess situations or hear responses to our questions. Some of us become Aesop, the man of morals; or Solomon, rendering wise solutions in a single phrase; or a professor, who can deliver a discourse at the drop of a hat; or the Little Red Hen, who instantly nags and hovers; or a clergyman, a preacher extraordinaire; or Methuselah, who usually begins his sentences with "when I was your age"; or a win-mongering coach who is always disappointed with less-than-perfect results and who motivates through fear and guilt; or the Grim Reaper, prognosticator of doom and despair.

If a person knows that an answer will trigger a lecture, guilt, or anger, more often than not he or she will not give an honest reply. I remember overhearing a father "interview" his child in a hallway. He was obviously angry, because his face was red and arteries stood out on his forehead. This father was definitely bold enough to ask his son the questions that apparently needed to be asked, but he was unable to keep quiet. "Are you involved in this type of thing?" he asked his son in angry tones. Without taking a breath or pausing, he continued: "Because if you are I'll tell you what, you're in deep trouble and . . ." I can't or care not to remember the rest of this man's conversation—with himself.

When I am approached by a youth who is struggling, I often ask, "Do your parents know about this?" They look at me as if I was from a different planet. Their eyes widen, and their faces become flushed. "Are you crazy? My parents would *kill* me!" I usually chuckle and tell them that their parents might *want* to kill them, but I seriously doubt they would actually do the deed. It intrigues me that children are afraid to tell adults that they have made a mistake for fear of punishment. Unfortunately, it is not just the mistakes they keep secret. They don't seem to want to tell parents about hobbies, interests, professional desires, dates, fears, or even if they are contemplating changing their major in college. "They will just never understand," I was once told by a college student who was unhappy in her major and wanted to pursue another course. "They are counting on me to be successful." Determined for her success, yes. Concerned with her happiness, unfortunately no.

It is not only important to foster a relationship that allows changes to occur, but it is imperative to help those we love understand our reactions in terms other than anger. If we are determined to build a relationship of trust, then we must build a relationship open to discussion. Lives can change with parental involvement. I marvel at those who describe their relationship with their parents in almost sacred tones. Some who talk about their parents are bolstered with enthusiasm, while others describe their respect in almost awestruck tones. I have been encouraged by the support of parents who have rallied behind their children in times of crisis and supported, encouraged, and even *understood* them. I love to see children be surprised when their parents demonstrate not anger but compassion and love as they nurse them in their trials. What a powerful lesson and witness of parenthood such parents are.

6. *Fathers must become fluent in "heart-speak," a language of love and testimony.* I've been in hundreds of classes in my lifetime. I must admit that some of these classes were more memorable than others. As I reflect upon memorable classroom experiences, I cannot always remember the exact thing taught, technique used, or visual displayed. I do, however, remember how I felt, usually with distinct clarity. These educational experiences made me feel almost as if I was invited into a new realm, a world where I belonged and connected. I attribute this sensation mostly to the teacher, although I realize that subject matter and teaching methods can contribute as well. While many aspects of a father's interview may appear mechanical, the most important element behind the whole process is the invitation to belong.

Joseph F. Smith expressed a father's invitation by saying: "Brethren, . . . if you will keep your [children] close to your heart, within the clasp of your arms; if you will make them to feel that you love them . . . and keep them near to you, they will not go very far from you, and they will not commit any very great sin. But it is when you turn them out of the home, turn them out of your affection— . . . that [is what] drives them from you." (*Gospel Doctrine,* 5th ed. [Salt Lake City: Deseret Book Co., 1939], pp. 281–82.) President Smith continued, "Fathers, if you wish your children to be taught in the principles of the gospel, if you wish them to love the truth and understand it, if you wish them to be obedient to and united with you, love them! and prove to them that you do love them by your every word and act to them" (ibid., p. 316). I can hardly think of a better time to express deep feelings between father and child than during a private heart-to-heart chat. When love illuminates the father's interview, it dispels the shadows of an awkward form, sticky situations, or feelings of distance.

Parental Councils

Once all the interviews are completed, the notes from the interviews serve as an excellent resource for a discussion of family welfare with your spouse. I believe you should always honor entrusted confidences, but generally the information obtained during your interviews can be used to help both you and your wife counsel on family matters. My wife and I gather together and laugh about some of the comments made by the younger children, yet at the same time we marvel at their growth and development. It is enlightening to discuss together our needed improvements as suggested by our children. By discussing interview outcomes together, we have become one in commitment and purpose. This unity is conveyed to our family in decisions, actions, and words. Even more important, our individual perspectives are combined to understand the needs of our family.

I am thoroughly convinced that if we as fathers exercise our stewardship by taking the time to interview our children regardless of their ages, memorable experiences will begin to permeate the hearts of our families. I am certain that what our families will remember will be our love and efforts. The fatherly interview serves as a pivotal foundation in establishing relationships and fulfilling the stewardship responsibility of the priesthood father. While you may not be ideally suited for interviewing or while your forms and techniques may need some revisions, at least your children will know that you are willing to try, that you care enough to take the time, and, most important, that you take your fatherly stewardship seriously.

6

Modeling

It was early in the afternoon as we stood in a narrow hallway in an old apartment building in Copenhagen. My companion on this first day of my mission knocked on the door, and we awaited the answer. I still couldn't believe I was in Europe. After all, Europe was so far away and so . . . European! Here I was in Denmark as a missionary, listening to a foreign language and tracting! I had heard about tracting all my life. We even practiced it in the missionary training center. But this experience was different from my older brothers' tracting stories, the missionary prep classes, and the role-playing at the MTC in Provo. It was much more intense to know that a *real* Dane with a *real* life was living behind the door, not my language teacher pretending to be a stubborn investigator. At last, missionary life in the trenches!

A man answered the door, and my companion introduced us. I marveled at how easy he made it look. He smiled as he spoke Danish, and he even answered the man's questions. My companion politely asked if we might come inside and teach an introductory lesson about our religion. It seemed so fluid! Although our request was declined and we moved to the next door, I was very impressed with my companion. He spoke with ease and looked comfortable. Obviously he knew what he was doing; after all, he had been in Denmark for almost five months! He pointed out some tracting ground rules and managed to give me good advice without sounding bossy. Then he showed me how it all worked by knocking on a few more doors. After five or six doors, my companion turned to me and announced, "Your turn!" My turn? He had to be kidding! My mind began to compile excuses. *I have just arrived in Denmark,* I thought. *I have jet lag and might fall asleep in the middle of a door approach.* It was inevitable that sooner or later I would need to take my turn, but I didn't feel adequate to take the plunge quite yet. "Please do a couple more," I pleaded. I watched intently as my companion knocked on the next few doors. I scrutinized every word and mannerism, for I knew my turn was coming.

Finally, the moment of truth arrived. I knocked and prayed. With the help of a patient companion, I managed to give a decent door approach. While my companion's suggestions, rules, and promptings were helpful, his demonstration of tracting in *real* missionary life was invaluable.

The greatest learning tool is observing. We can be told something a thousand times and feel that we have a pretty good idea about the subject, but to personally witness the subject ourselves is far more beneficial. It has been said that a picture paints a thousand words. While looking at the picture adds dimension and color, being in the picture adds depth, smell, and reality. There is an enhanced quality about personally experiencing something while being tutored, coached, or even just taken along for the ride. It seems that we glean values in addition to just techniques as we travel along life's path. We learn to talk by listening to others talk and then mimicking what we hear. We learn by reading all we can, watching others, and analyzing their techniques, and then we jump into the world by mimicking what we have read, studied, and observed.

Observing something firsthand has a powerful effect upon us. This way of learning can confirm our existing beliefs, validate our actions or hunches, and promote change. Perhaps the following example will illustrate my point. I have always considered myself patriotic. I suspect this had a lot to do with my parents and their feelings for the United States, although I cannot ever remember having lessons on patriotism or being told how Americans are patriotic. I saw numerous pictures of Old Glory in history books and on postcards and posters during my youth. I thought it was neat to see holes in the flag from the cannon fire and scorched edges from the flames of the "perilous fight." Yet somewhere amidst all the history lessons, my father's war stories, my mother's standing with everyone else when the flag passed by in a parade, and a thousand recitations of the Pledge of Allegiance, I learned what patriotism was and it became part of me. One morning, I was moved quite unexpectedly as I stood in one of the Smithsonian buildings in Washington, D.C., and listened to "The Star-Spangled Banner" as Old Glory was slowly raised. It was a moment I shall never forget. It transcended every picture, preconceived notion, and description of Old Glory I had ever seen or heard. It was an endearing memory as well as enduring.

When it comes to fatherhood, having a good example is paramount. Good fathers provide us models to mimic. But what do we see today? What types of fathers are serving as models for future generations? President Howard W. Hunter said that "we live in a world that seems to worship its own kind of greatness and produce its own kind of heroes" ("What Is True Greatness?" in *Brigham Young University 1986–87 Devotional and Fireside Speeches* [Provo, Utah: University Publications, 1987], p.111).

Unfortunately, the models of the world adhere to principles of little value, which generally produce meaningless outcomes and consequences. In 1905 President Joseph F. Smith warned the Saints about the worldly standards we accept and emulate. He wrote: "Those things which we call extraordinary, remarkable, or unusual may make history, but they do not make real life. After all, to do well those things which God ordained to be the common lot of all mankind, is the truest greatness. To be a successful father or a successful mother is greater than to be a successful general or a successful statesman." ("Common-place Things," *Juvenile Instructor,* 15 December 1905, p. 752.) President Smith then concluded: "Let us not be trying to substitute an artificial life for the true one" (ibid., p. 753).

In the constant contest to keep up with the world, we often lose sight of the most important elements of our lives. This was exemplified in Lehi's vision of the tree of life. One group of people pressed forward, holding fast to the iron rod until they arrived at the tree and partook of the fruit. Yet after they had eaten the fruit, they acted as if they were ashamed (see 1 Nephi 8:24–25). Lehi didn't understand this reaction, which was foreign to his own experience; when he had partaken of the fruit, he was filled with "exceedingly great joy" (1 Nephi 8:12). Puzzled by their ashamed reaction, Lehi cast his eyes round about and noticed a great and spacious building that was filled with the wisdom and pride of the world (see 1 Nephi 11:35–36). As those partakers of the fruit paid attention to what the world was saying, listened to their mocking voices, and noticed their scornful fingers pointing, they were ashamed of their righteous actions and "fell away into forbidden paths and were lost" (1 Nephi 8:28).

As we mimic the world's model of living, those things which should command our attention are moved to the periphery. Eventually these peripheral objects become nothing more than vague memories of the past. Elder A. Theodore Tuttle taught: "Our most flagrant violations, perhaps, occur in our own homes. We chase worldly pleasures and neglect our own innocent children. . . . The trials through which today's young people are passing—ease and luxury—may be the most severe test of any age. Brothers and sisters, stay close to your own! Guide them safely! These are perilous times. Give increased attention. Give increased effort." (In Conference Report, October 1971, p. 95.) The time has come to model a proper standard of fatherhood. Modeling any standard requires the mentor to reflect the desired standard. Bishop H. Burke Peterson felt that "we will be effective as fathers only as our lives reflect what we wish to teach." He also said, "Remember, fathers, you are always teaching—for good or for ill." ("The Father's Duty to Foster the Welfare of His Family," *Ensign,* November 1977, p. 88.)

Personal Consistency

As a teacher, I have noticed some students who have learned the system well enough that they can answer almost any question. It's not that they have acquired superior knowledge; it's just that they have learned the type of answers teachers want to hear. Giving such an answer doesn't require thought, for these responses neatly answer almost any question. From a religious standpoint, these versatile answers are often called "Sunday School answers." I'm sure that you are familiar with Sunday School answers. Here's how they work. Suppose that in a Sunday School class the teacher asks a question. It really doesn't matter what the question is, because a Sunday School answer has such range and versatility that it would fit any reasonable religious question. "What should you do when faced with a personal crisis?" the teacher asks. Without thinking, we fill in the answer. "Pray," one member mentions. "Have faith," another might say. While these answers are correct, they become rote blurbs rather than explanations of practiced realities.

As we become more knowledgeable about gospel terms and the right answers, we face a danger of saying the right thing but doing the opposite. For example, I overheard a frustrated woman standing in line at a grocery store checkout reprimand one of her children. Apparently there had been a scuffle between the two children sitting in the shopping cart. The mother grabbed the child's hand and began slapping it. "We do not hit, we do not hit," she repeated each time she slapped the child's hand. This experience left me numb. I was taken aback by the spirit of the event, but most annoying was the contradiction of the whole situation. What message was being modeled? Perhaps the greatest teaching tool is consistency.

As fathers, most of us know what should be done. We can give the right answers and say the right thing: "Family comes first." "You can talk to me anytime." "You are the most impor-tant thing in my life." If our practice, however, does not match the message, the message loses power and meaning, becoming nothing more than words. A priesthood father can never lead others into the celestial kingdom if he is not bound for the same destination. One does not pass through the celestial kingdom while enroute to another destination. As we muddle our way through mortality and its pitfalls, successful and consistent behavior should be the rule rather than the exception.

Perhaps that is why the Lord has admonished us to set our own houses in order (see D&C 88:119). I will never forget one experience I had as a teenager. A friend and I walked to his house one evening. As we entered through the kitchen door, my friend's father came rushing into the kitchen and confronted him. Apparently, my friend had failed to follow through on doing something his father had asked him to do. This father was livid, and I was embarrassed and wanted to leave. Unfortunately, I was trapped in the corner of the kitchen with the father and son between me and the door. My body tensed as emotions escalated and my friend's father began shouting. I stood silently in the corner not knowing what to do. This father reminded his son how he couldn't be trusted and how irresponsible he was. In frustration, my friend interrupted his father by blurting out, "Dad, is this another one of your 'do as I say and not as I do' lectures?" I thought at this point that I was about to witness a homicide. It was common knowledge that my friend's dad was not very dependable, that he struggled to maintain his own avowed standards and was brash. As I stood frozen in the corner hoping to somehow blend into the wallpaper, to my amazement the room fell silent. The father hung his head and quietly retreated to his bedroom. I shot a glance at my friend, expecting a smile of relief. Instead, his head also hung, and I noticed tears rolling down his cheeks. I realized then the importance of words and practice. Power comes when consistency becomes our pattern. As fathers, we owe our children an example of doing what we say. "Before [a father] can produce the work of sa[n]ctification in his family," Brigham Young advised, "he must sanctify himself, and by this means God can help him to sanctify his family" (in *Journal of Discourses,* 9:283).

Marriage

President David O. McKay counseled, "A father can do no greater thing for his children than to let them feel that he loves their mother" (quoted by Elder Gordon B. Hinckley in Conference Report, April 1971, p. 82). Marriage is becoming a dinosaur of sorts in modern society. Some view marriage as cumbersome, others feel it is an outdated institution, and some think it is already extinct. One of my greatest concerns prior to my marriage was the continually rising divorce percentage, a statistic the doomsayers proclaim as if nothing can be done about it. Those who are not yet married constantly wrestle with this type of adverse news concerning marriage. While the divorce rates are indeed rising, singles need to know that there are still many healthy, happy marriages in the world. Models of happy marriages are imperative for those overwhelmed by the prognosticators of failure.

A proper model of marriage can be a lifeline for those who recognize the decaying relationships of today but who are still desperately seeking a happy marriage. It is surprising to me how even little things make significant impressions upon others. For example, not long ago I was talking with a group of teens between sessions at a youth conference. One individual told a blonde joke. This led to another blonde joke, and another, and another. After several blonde jokes, I said with a smile, "Now, be careful—my wife's a blonde." Following my next presentation, I noticed a young lady waiting to talk with me. With tears welling up in her eyes, she said: "I just wanted to thank you for standing up for your wife. It's nice to know that men still feel that way about their wives today." At first my mind raced through my last talk to pinpoint something I had said about my wife. Then it dawned on me that she was part of the group I was talking to prior to my lecture; the young woman was referring to my statement about my wife being blonde. As I thought back upon my statement, I recognized that I really wasn't that gallant. But if this young woman had seen marriage modeled only in a demeaning or critical way, no wonder my comment was significant to her. I wonder if the practice of chivalry has really become so uncommon. Obviously we need more examples of good marriages for our youth to observe.

It is your responsibility to build a loving relationship in your marriage. We should let our children know of our love not only for them but for their mother as well. You should tell your children about your love for your wife, speak of their mother in cherished tones, and be respectful of her character. It helps for those being mentored in marriage to understand the broad spectrum of feelings in marriage, so share the feelings you had for your wife when you first met. Once, as our family drove home from a vacation, my daughter enthusiastically called out, "Everyone put your hand over your heart!" We complied. Megan then explained, "This is where Mom and Dad first held hands!" Sure enough, we had passed the very spot where Lisa and I first held hands during our courtship. Megan then proceeded to tell us the whole story in full detail. I watched her in the rearview mirror as I was driving. She was filled with enthusiasm and laughter. I was not as impressed that she could remember all the details as that she *would* remember.

As we model happy marriages, seeds of a happy marriage are planted in the hearts of those we mentor. As with any harvest, it takes time for the seeds to grow, mature, and bear fruit. I believe in the harvesting of seeds sowed in youth. Many times we will never realize the power of planting seeds in the lives of others. In Proverbs we read: "Who can find a virtuous woman? for her price is far above rubies. The heart of her husband doth safely trust in her, so that he shall have no need of spoil. . . . Her children arise up, and call her blessed; her husband also, and he praiseth her." (Proverbs 31:10–11, 28.) I often make notes in the margins of my scriptures. In the margin next to this scripture, a note reads, "Lisa Jeanne—Amen!" In my estimation, my wife, Lisa Jeanne, is aptly described in these verses. If the scripture fits, wear it! This note of mine was actually a harvesting of a seed planted years before I met Lisa. At a very young and impressionable age, I was looking for a story in a set of scriptures I happened to find in our living room. As I was thumbing through the pages, I happened to come across Proverbs 31. In the margin a note in my *father's* handwriting read, "Andy," which was my dad's nickname for my mother, Andrea. Without his knowing, what I learned from my father was the feelings a husband could have for his wife. The seeds from a loving marriage can be constantly sown in hopes of a fruitful harvest in generations to come.

Elder James E. Faust urged "each husband and father of this Church to be the kind of man your wife would not want to be without. I urge the sisters of this Church to be patient, loving, and understanding with their husbands. Those who enter into marriage should be fully prepared to establish their marriage as the first priority in their lives." (In Conference Report, April 1993, p. 46.) As we listen to Elder Faust's inspired counsel, I can't help but hear the words of James echo in my heart and mind: "Be ye doers of the word, and not hearers only" (James 1:22). Making this advice work in our marriages is a difficult task.

Paul called marriage one of the great mysteries (see Ephesians 5:31–32). A mystery is a truth that can be known only through revelation. It makes sense that Paul would call marriage a mystery, because it can be understood only through revelation. Paul stated that marriage was the joining of two separate individuals into "one flesh" (Ephesians 5:31). In our marriage we should model a oneness by being partners. "Your wife is your partner in the leadership of the family," Elder Boyd K. Packer said, "and should have full knowledge of and full participation in all decisions relating to your home" (in Conference Report, April 1994, p. 26).

As marriage partners are yoked together, they both pull the weight of the family responsibility. They share decisions as well as discipline. Great power comes from a marriage wherein the partners work together and model unity. This power comes not just through words but as both partners demonstrate their partnership in practice. Perhaps the following example will illustrate the power of partnership.

My father always stressed integrity in our home. As a matter of fact, his trademark was his personal integrity. I listened to the stories, morals, and lessons my father taught our family as I was growing up. More important, my father never gave me reason to doubt that his practice was not in harmony with his teachings. Like my father, my mother believed in integrity, but it was my father who seemed to talk about it. It was almost as if this was "Dad's thing." I learned the importance of integrity, however, through witnessing the partnership of my father and mother.

When I was in seventh grade, I was elected president of my class. After the announcement of the new class officers, some of the other elected officers mentioned to me that they were all going roller-skating that night at the local skating rink in celebration. Excited to be part of the new group, I immediately accepted their invitation. Later that evening, as I was waiting for my ride to the roller-skating rink, my mother reminded me of a birthday party I had previously committed to attend. Without telling my mother about the roller-skating celebration, I decided to go roller-skating rather than attend the birthday party.

Not long after we arrived at the skating rink, an announcement was made for all the girls to go to one side of the rink and all the boys to go to the opposite side. It was time for the "snowball," an activity in which one boy and one girl would skate to the opposite end of the rink and choose a partner to skate with. At the cue, the couples would break and each would then choose another partner. This would continue until it "snowballed" into a large group with everyone skating. I must admit it sounds rather childish, but to a seventh grader this was high adventure! After the rules were explained over the loudspeakers, the houselights were dimmed and the mirror ball began spinning, casting spots throughout the rink. As we waited for the music to begin, I saw a silhouetted figure walking across the floor. Since this person was not wearing skates, I thought it must be the manager coming out to start the activity. This person didn't walk like a manager, however, but more like a person on a mission: leaning slightly forward, taking purposeful steps, and moving fast. As this figure came closer, I realized that it wasn't the manager of the skating rink. To my horror, I realized that it was my mother!

Almost in military cadence, my mother marched right up to me, grabbed me by my arm, and said, "Come with me, young man!" I was familiar enough with my mother's vocabulary to know that anytime you were called by your full name or addressed as "young man," you were in serious trouble. She marched me across the roller-skating rink and sat me down on a bench. "Change your skates," she said. "We're leaving." I hurriedly changed into my shoes and was promptly escorted out of the rink, flushed with embarrassment. I had never been more mortified in all my twelve years of life! Didn't my mother realize that these were my new friends? Didn't she understand that popularity was a fragile venture? Did she know that she had just ended my prospects for any semblance of a normal seventh-grade experience?

We didn't speak as she drove. I just looked out the window and grunted occasionally so she would know how upset I was. Rather than driving home, my mother drove straight to the birthday party I had originally committed to attend. She handed me a gift, reminded me to be a gentleman, and told me to get out of the car and go to the party. I was shocked. This was so embarrassing! Right before I slammed the car door shut, I told my mother that I would never speak to her again.

After the party, I walked home. As I walked into the house,

my parents were sitting at the kitchen table. In silence I strode past them and went straight to my bedroom. As I lay in bed, I knew my parents were probably beside themselves questioning whether Mom's actions were appropriate or not. Maybe they were crying and lamenting that they had disjointed my young social life and scarred me for eternity. Now that I am a parent, when I reflect back on that experience I realize that my parents were probably giggling themselves silly as my mom told my father the whole story. By the way, I did speak to my mother again the very next morning—after all, I was hungry!

In time I began to realize something important about that experience. Whereas I once had been mortified by my mother's actions, I learned to cherish her decision. Of course, I came to understand the error in my judgment of not honoring my previous commitment to the birthday party. My father's lessons and examples made that clear; all I could think of was, "My word is my bond." It was the combination of my father's lessons and my mother's determined raid of Rollercity that forever riveted the importance of integrity onto my soul. I knew my father and mother were united and that their partnership was lasting. Integrity wasn't just my father's hobby; it was my parents' value. The experience of witnessing their partnership in power has forever altered my life. I am indebted and grateful to have learned such important principles at such an early age. Alma would have been proud of me for learning wisdom in my youth (see Alma 37:35). I hope that I will have enough courage to march across a roller-skating rink to teach important principles to my children—I know my partner will!

A Covenant Relationship

Although my roller-skating incident was a powerful lesson in modeling partnership in marriage, there is something even more important that should be modeled in a marriage. I have concluded that as we begin to understand the mystery of marriage as revealed by God, we realize that marriage builds upon partnership to bring us to a deeper principle: a covenant relationship. Herein lies the mystery and power of marriage as demonstrated in Ecclesiastes 4:9–12. This scripture extols the benefits of a partnership. "Two are better than one; because they have a good reward for their labour. For if they fall, the one will lift up his fellow: but woe to him that is alone when he falleth; for he hath not another to help him up. Again, if two lie together, then they have heat: but how can one be warm alone? And if one prevail against him, two shall withstand him." This all makes perfect sense. It is obvious that the work of many hands is more productive than singular effort. Partnership offers protection, warmth, security, and lighter work.

The power of a real relationship, however, is emphasized in the very last line of verse 12: "And a *three*fold cord is not quickly broken." It is interesting that while these verses point out the benefits of partnership between two people, the emphasis is really on "three" individuals and not two. Maybe this was a mathematical glitch or a translation error. Maybe it should have said "a *two*fold cord is not quickly broken." But I believe that this verse is not an error but a blessing. What is the threefold cord? The husband is one of the cords, the wife is the other, and the power and covenant are bound up by a third cord: Jesus Christ. Marriage partners who work together as a partnership can expect the benefits of partnership. As we intertwine Christ in our partnership of marriage, we can also reap protection, inspiration, and increased love. Christ becomes a part of our union through our marriage covenants.

This covenant relationship is the ideal that every family can and should achieve. The lasting legacy of everlasting covenants must not only be taught but also demonstrated. As we weave divinity into our marriages, we begin to see heaven on earth. Elder James E. Faust said: "I wonder if it is possible for one marriage partner to jettison the other and become completely whole. Either partner who diminishes the divine role of the other in the presence of the children demeans the budding femininity within the daughters and the emerging manhood of the sons." (In Conference Report, April 1993, p. 46.) Families of covenant relationships work to model values of charity and unity.

Home of the Spirit

President Ezra Taft Benson invited us to provide a home where love and the Spirit of the Lord can abide as we teach principles of truth. He said, "One great thing the Lord requires of each of us is to provide a home where a happy, positive influence for good exists" (in Conference Report, April 1981, p. 46). So important is a happy home that Joseph Smith, Sidney Rigdon, and Frederick G. Williams were rebuked by the Lord concerning their families. On May 6, 1833, in Kirtland, Ohio, the Lord reminded these brethren, "I have commanded you to bring up your children in light and truth" (D&C 93:40). Then each of the men was in turn reminded of his family responsibilities and charged to "set in order" his house (D&C 93:41–48). A. Theodore Tuttle once asked: "How would you pass the test, parents, if your family was isolated from the Church and *you* had to supply all religious training? Have you become so dependent on others that you do little or nothing at home? Tell me, how much of the *gospel* would your children know, if all they knew is what they had been taught at home?" (In Conference Report, October 1979, p. 39.) This is a staggering thought. I am forever grateful for the instruction my family has received at the hand of the Church, and I hope that such resources will always be available to my family members. But Elder Tuttle's remarks ring a clarion call for all families to lay foundations and teach the gospel.

In light of both President Benson's call for a happy home and Elder Tuttle's reminder of the importance of teaching the gospel, we have been encouraged to build our families through family home evening and family scripture study and prayer.

Family Home Evening

When we were first married, my wife and I decided that we wanted a family that would be close to the gospel and be active in obtaining the Lord's blessings. A familiar quote by Elder Boyd K. Packer about family home evening became part of our family plan to accomplish our goal: "With this program comes the promise from the prophets, the living prophets, that if parents will gather their children about them once a week and teach the gospel, those children in such families will not go astray" (in Conference Report, October 1970, p. 121).

It is easy to see how that noble promise caught our attention. Since we both firmly believe in the power of prophetic word, Elder Packer's promise was good enough for us! We decided that we would begin to lay claim upon Elder Packer's promise early, from the beginning of our marriage. Lisa and I committed to hold regular weekly family home evenings. In theory, that should have been easy. How difficult could it be to hold a family home evening with just my wife and me? In reality, however, we discovered some interesting challenges. For instance, we felt a temptation to wait for our family to expand before we held family night. I remember sitting in our miniature basement apartment on Monday evenings preparing to have family night. "Let's have an opening prayer," I suggested. "Who should I call on *this* time?" We would roll our eyes and laugh. Lisa would say the prayer, and I would give the lesson—and the next Monday we would switch assignments. We understood the importance of family home evening, but we found a temptation to do only activities during this stage in our lives. Our motto could have been "Build our family relationships—through fun!"

This is a subtle trap. Granted, family activities build relationships and are vital to the overall workings of a family, but we discovered an important condition of Elder Packer's advice. His prophetic promise that our children will not go astray does not apply if we go bowling once a week, or sledding, or watch videos—it applies if we "teach the gospel." Activities are important, but teaching is the critical part of the family home evening experience.

Family home evening was first introduced to the Church membership in 1915. Family home evening is often interpreted as good social advice, but it is more than just a social program. It is a divinely inspired program that carries prophetic promises even beyond Elder Packer's. The First Presidency issued the following statement concerning family home evening: "If the Saints obey this counsel, we promise that great blessings will result. Love at home and obedience to parents will increase. Faith will be developed in the hearts of the youth of Israel, and they will gain power to combat the evil influence and temptations which beset them." (James R. Clark, comp., *Messages of the First Presidency,* 6 vols. [Salt Lake City: Bookcraft, 1965–75], 4:339; see also Harold B. Lee, *Ye Are the Light of the World* [Salt Lake City: Deseret Book Co., 1974], p. 82.) President Joseph F. Smith promised that "not one child in a hundred would go astray, if the home environment, example and training, were in harmony with the truth in the gospel of Christ, as revealed and taught to the Latter-day Saints" (Gospel Doctrine, 5th ed. [Salt Lake City: Deseret Book Co., 1939], p. 302). Long before 1915 prophets consistently instructed families about the necessity of gospel-centered homes and proper gospel instruction. For example, in Proverbs 22:6 we read, "Train up a child in the way he should go: and when he is old, he will not depart from it."

Two important elements are stressed in prophetic promises. First, family home evening must be held regularly. Family gatherings should be the rule rather than the exception. When family home evening becomes the rule, it provides a family with tradition, security, and protection. We have been instructed to gather our families together weekly. Elder L. Tom Perry said that "family home evenings are for everyone, whether it be in a two-parent home, a single-parent home, or in a single-member family unit" (in Conference Report, April 1994, p. 50).

Second, family home evening is a time for instruction. It is clear that teaching our families the proper way by modeling is invaluable. President Harold B. Lee said, "Teach your families in your family home evening, teach them to keep the commandments of God, for therein is our only safety in these days!" (In Conference Report, April 1973, p. 181.) Some families may try to lay claim to the prophetic promises by merely gathering together for short devotionals or family activities. While these activities are good and have their benefits and rewards, the prophetic promises stress teaching. "Regarding our home evenings," President Spencer W. Kimball said, "An evening home with the family or an evening out to some place of interest with your family only partly solves the need of the home evening. Basically important is the teaching of the children the way of life that is vitally important. Merely going to a show or a party together, or fishing, only half satisfies the real need, but to stay home and *teach* the children the gospel, the scriptures, and love for each other and love for their parents is most important." (In Conference Report, October 1977, p. 4; emphasis added.)

After we come to a realization of the specific nature of the prophetic promises about family home evening, it is important we evaluate our current practice according to the instructions of the Lord. Perhaps some of us need to start *having* family home evenings, while others need to make them more regular or tune-up their content. Each family should consider ways of making their home evenings a time of building traditions, relationships, spirituality, and gospel knowledge.

Elder Marion D. Hanks said, "How foolish we are if we reserve to ourselves, or for others than our own children, the knowledge and testimony of the gospel we have gained. They, no less than others, need and deserve this from us." (In Conference Report, April 1974, p. 112.) Elder Hanks's comment made an impact on my family and caused us to reflect upon our family practices. We have always made a point to have a lesson in our home evenings, but Elder Hanks's inspired teaching has helped us stretch. Perhaps the following story will illustrate what I mean. While preparing at the missionary training center for my mission, I pored over the missionary discussions in preparation for teaching in the mission field. As I studied the lessons, a familiar pattern emerged throughout them: teach a principle of the gospel and then bear personal testimony of its truthfulness. I never fully realized the power of this pattern until I was actually teaching investigators. Truth combined with personal testimony results in divine power—I really can't explain it any better than that. While my wife and I were teaching gospel principles in our family home evenings, we felt that we were lacking the power of personal testimony. As I thought more about this, I realized that Elder Hanks was right; we were reserving our testimony for ourselves or others. I remember hearing my parents and siblings bear their testimonies, but only in a testimony meeting or at youth conference. A testimony is a sacred and meaningful outpouring of the soul. When it is shared, it can dissolve misunderstandings, heal wounded hearts, strengthen faith, and encourage a disappointed spirit. Why then do we reserve it for others and rarely share it with those we love most?

We decided we needed to bear our testimonies to each other in family home evenings. Testimonies have become an essential part of our family home evening assignment schedule, which includes opening prayer, song, lesson, testimony, and Article of Faith. I am grateful for Elder Hanks's advice. This obvious but overlooked element has changed the spirit and effectiveness of our family home evenings. It is a wonderful feeling to hear siblings express their love of God, family, and each other in our own home as directed by the Spirit.

Not only does bearing testimonies strengthen the spirituality of the home, but it teaches younger children what a testimony is and gives them a chance to express their feelings. I find it far more comfortable to coach my three-year-old while bearing her testimony in my home than in public settings. For example, recently it was my youngest daughter's turn to bear her testimony in home evening. "It is now Lauren's turn to bear her testimony," I said after the lesson was finished. "Okay!" she said and enthusiastically jumped up. "I'd like to bear my testimony," she said confidently. As she stood poised to continue, she paused, shuffled, and then got a blank look on her face. Sheepishly she looked at me and said, "How do I do this again?" I invited her to stand by my chair, and then I explained that a testimony is something we believe or know. "Do you believe or love anything, Lauren?" "Yes, Dad," she replied. "What?" She thought for a moment and then said something like, "I love my family." "Okay," I said, "why don't you tell our family that?" "I love my family," Lauren said with a big smile. "Do you know anything else? Do you have any other feelings?" I asked. "Do you believe in prophets?" "Oh, yes," she answered. "Maybe you should tell the family that part too." "I know Gordon B. Hinckley [she o-ver e-nun-ci-at-ed every syllable in President Hinckley's name in the way only three-year-olds can do] is a prophet." While this process was a little time-consuming, it was a wonderful teaching moment and a great experience for me, my family, and Lauren. My children deserve to hear the gospel taught in their own home, and they also deserve to know that their father and other family members know it is true as well.

Family Scripture Study

Every family should study the words of Christ. Like interviews, scripture study feels right, makes sense, and rings with truth. But getting going is often difficult. I worry that some families forego scripture study because they are not quite sure if they are doing it right. Bishop H. Burke Peterson commented on this subject: "There shouldn't be—there mustn't be—one family in this Church that doesn't take the time to read from the scriptures every day. Every family can do it in their own way." (In Conference Report, April 1975, p. 79.) I have heard presentation after presentation about the so-called right way to study the scriptures, but I agree with Elder Peterson that the important thing is having the scriptures become part of your family. Therefore, consider your family's needs, such as your children's ages and maturity levels. Many resources are available to help your scripture study, but the scriptures themselves possess a power that is unique. We have no reason to fear the scriptural text, for when we study it with the power of the Holy Ghost, testimonies are born, feelings are stirred, and perspective is renewed. Elder Dean L. Larsen believes "there is special power in the scriptures" (in Conference Report, October 1989, p. 77). I too believe that with all my heart.

Family Prayer

Christ taught the Nephites, "Therefore blessed are ye if ye shall keep my commandments, which the Father hath commanded me that I should give unto you" (3 Nephi 18:14). The first commandment the Lord discusses following this statement is prayer. He tells us to "pray in your families unto the Father, always in my name, that your wives and your children may be blessed" (3 Nephi 18:21). Elder John H. Groberg said, "If we truly love our families we will constantly pray for them and with them. I know of no single activity that has more potential for unifying our families and bringing more love and divine direction into our homes than consistent, fervent family prayer." (In Conference Report, April 1982, p. 75.) A question that often arises concerning family prayer (or family home evening) is "what exactly constitutes a family?"

Prior to my marriage in the Salt Lake Temple, I listened intently to advice given to us by Elder Carlos E. Asay. His counsel made a deep impression upon me and my wife, and we have cherished his words of encouragement and testimony, particularly regarding prayer. He counseled us to never let a day pass without kneeling together in prayer. I can still remember him raising the tone of his voice slightly and saying, "Starting tonight!" This inspired counsel has become a legacy in our home. In order that we would never forget whose turn it was to offer our couple prayer, we decided that I would offer prayers on the odd dates of the month and my wife would pray on the even dates. I have often wondered if my designation of the odd dates of the month was indicative of my character. Nevertheless, this simple formula has served its purpose.

As families grow, praying together as a family becomes equally important. Just as praying together as a couple does not replace our personal prayers, family prayers do not replace praying together as husband and wife. Family prayer augments our spiritual practice rather than replaces it. President Heber J. Grant once said, "I am convinced that one of the greatest things that can come into any home to cause the boys and girls in that home to grow up in a love of God, and in a love of the gospel of Jesus Christ, is to have family prayer" (*Gospel Standards,* comp. G. Homer Durham [Salt Lake City: *Improvement Era,* 1941], p. 25). Family prayer not only expresses our supplication and gratitude to Heavenly Father but also builds our family unity and solidarity. President Kimball described family prayer as a "moment when the world is shut out and heaven enclosed within" (Edward L. Kimball, ed., *The Teachings of Spencer W. Kimball* [Salt Lake City: Bookcraft, 1982], p. 116).

Fathers have the responsibility to gather the family together. President Kimball said, "When we kneel in family prayer, our children at our side on their knees are learning habits that will stay with them all through their lives" (ibid., pp. 117–118). It is also our responsibility to teach our children to pray. Few joys are greater than kneeling beside your children as they learn to say their personal prayers. I must admit, however, that on many occasions I have been the student while listening to my children offer their personal prayers.

For those whose children have long since left your home, prayer should still be the mortar of your home. We never out-grow personal prayer, and as long as we are married we are bound to pray as a couple. President Kimball also admonished us to encourage others to pray as families (see ibid., p. 117). I remember as a boy often hearing my parents tell me, "Don't for-get to say your prayers!" after I told them good night. That very phrase is heard in my home today. It has become a legacy of faith. Fathers should often remind and encourage their grown children and grandchildren to not forget to say their prayers. Elder Groberg advised, "No matter what other inheritance you leave your family, give them the inheritance of knowing through experience that, forever, you will be praying for them and they for you" (in Conference Report, April 1982, p. 117).

7

Taking the Brakes Off

In a hurry to get up the canyon, my friend and I jumped into the car and started up the long scenic road. The climb was gradual. While the car seemed to operate normally, something was subtly wrong. Obviously it is difficult for a car to accelerate up a steep grade, but there was something *else* wrong. Nevertheless, we forged ahead up the winding canyon. "Do you smell something?" I inquired. Although the air was pungent, we couldn't quite place the odor. As the grade continued to steepen, the car strained even more. It felt as if we were towing all the cars behind us up the mountain (by the way, there was now a considerable number of cars behind us). Cars began passing us. We finally pulled to the side of the road to determine the problem. After looking under the hood, twisting knobs, pulling on wires, general fidgeting, and kicking all the tires, we couldn't find a problem; everything seemed to be in perfect working order. As we got into the car, we decided it would be best to return home. As my friend put the car into gear, we suddenly discovered the problem: the parking brake was on. Once the brake was released, our drive up the canyon was much easier. We still had the expected strain of climbing the canyon grade, but in comparison it was almost a breeze.

Elder Jeffrey R. Holland has said, "Brethren, we all know fatherhood is not an easy assignment, but it ranks among the most imperative ever given, in time or eternity" (in Conference Report, April 1983, p. 53). Although fatherhood is a difficult assignment, it is not an impossible task. Perhaps we can compare fatherhood to my canyon climb. Like the strain of climbing a steep grade, fatherhood can be difficult at times. It requires effort; you cannot just coast. Certain things, however, actually brake our efforts, making the climb even more laborious. As we address fatherhood, it is important to understand that we can do something about some things and yet other things we cannot help. Instead of exerting our efforts on the unchangeable things, we should concentrate on discovering which fatherhood brakes are inadvertently set in our own lives and then work at taking those brakes off.

The Unchangeable Hill

In my simple analogy, the grade of the hill represents those things we really can't change. These obstacles may include the realities of making a living, the limitations of only twenty-four hours in a day, and events of the past that have permanently changed the present and the future. As much as we would like to spend our prime hours with our family, the logistics of society dictate that we work during the prime hours of the day and make do with whatever else is left. Far too often, we spend most of our efforts working or worrying about those things we cannot change. For example, some fathers spend most of their time and efforts trying to make up for lost time rather than focusing on making the best of the present. Too many fathers try to make up for their past absences or times of neglect rather than acknowledging the mistake and then striving to be a good father now. Herein lies the hope: We can make changes, despite the past. President Kimball wrote these powerful, hopeful lines: "Man can transform himself and he must. Man has in himself the seeds of godhood, which can germinate and grow and develop. As the acorn becomes the oak, the mortal man becomes a god. It is within his power to lift himself by his very bootstraps from the plane on which he finds himself to the plane on which he should be. It may be a long, hard lift with many obstacles, but it is a real possibility." (Edward L. Kimball, ed., *The Teachings of Spencer W. Kimball* [Salt Lake City: Bookcraft, 1982], p. 28.)

Removing the Brakes

The ascent up fatherhood's slope is often hindered by things we can do something about. Too many fathers who realize that something is wrong in their progression as fathers fail to take off the parking brake or remove an obstacle from the path of progression. As we focus on the things we can do as fathers, we find more satisfaction and joy within our families.

Set the vision. One Sunday morning I went into my nine-year-old son's bedroom to wake him for our church meetings. "Dad," he asked, rubbing his eyes as he sat up in bed, "what's today?" "Sunday," I said matter-of-factly. He immediately began to groan. "What's wrong with Sunday?" I asked, as if I had no idea what was going through his young mind. At first he was reluctant to say anything, but then he got it off his chest: "Church lasts so long, and it's . . . it's . . . so *boring!*" As he spoke, I watched him writhe on his bed as if he were in pain. Finally I asked, "Zach, do you know why we go to church?" He sat there for a moment in silence. He didn't move, he didn't blink—he was frozen. I think my question overloaded his brain. I guess it had never occurred to him that we did things for a reason.

This experience startled me. It dawned on me that my children knew our family traditions, rules, and activities but that they really didn't understand why we did or didn't do certain things. They really didn't see what we were trying to accomplish as a family. As a matter of fact, they knew more about the United States Constitution than they knew about our family. We decided that we needed to be more specific with our children and let them know the reasons we have rules in the family and why we go to church, visit extended family, and hold family home evenings. We wanted our children to know what it meant to be a Richardson, so we decided to frame the Richardson Family Constitution. Similar to a mission statement, the family constitution is our declaration of what it means to be a member of our family.

We talked about framing the constitution in family home evening one Monday night. The kids thought it was a great idea. We decided it must be done as a family from start to finish. The only other requirement was that every family member had to agree on every item in the final document. That sounded easy enough. I naively sat with pencil and paper in hand and acted as scribe. After listening to all the ideas offered, we got a good feel for what we wanted to accomplish in our family. The key desire of our constitution was to increase our spirituality. So we wrote that desire at the top of the paper. "Now," I said, "what must we do as a family to make sure this desire will actually happen?" I wrote down suggestions that fit neatly into eight categories: physical, attitude, spirituality, having fun, effective communication, education, family traditions, and family environment. Working out the details, agreeing on the concepts, and making sure the constitution reflected our greatest desire took a little over one year.

As the months went by, I wondered if we were doing something wrong. Was our constitution too short or too long? There came a time when I wondered if the focus was too idealistic. Around this time I read Elder Packer's conference address in which he related, in essence, that some members wonder if the leaders of the Church realize that when they speak of Church ideals, some members are hurt by their plain-spoken words. I was impressed by the spirit and words of Elder Packer's reply: "Because we *do* know and because we *do* care, we must teach the rules of happiness without dilution, apology, or avoidance" (in Conference Report, April 1994, p. 25; emphasis in original). This gave our family the courage to keep our constitution intact. It really didn't matter if it was "too this" or "too that." It reflected our desires, represented our ideals, set the vision of the Richardson family—and it was ours.

Some unexpected benefits came as we worked together on defining our family. As the time drew closer for the signing of the Richardson Family Constitution, the excitement grew. Our children wanted to dress up like members of the Continental Congress on the day we signed our final document. At first I thought they were just teasing, but as I stood in my knickers, bow tie, and overcoat to sign my name on our constitution, I realized they too had certain expectations. I have been happy to hear references to our constitution made during everyday conversation. For example, one of the principles contained in our constitution is that "we are willing to try new experiences." It has been fun to see the children remind each other to try new foods at the dinner table. All they say are two words: "family constitution!" Enough said! Everyone adds a *small* sample of a "new experience" onto his or her plate. If you understand where you want to go, it is easier to define what happens between point A and point B. The vision of the family is vital. I'm reminded of Proverbs 29:18: "Where there is no vision, the people perish."

Establish priorities. Christ taught the establishment of priorities in a succinct and meaningful way in both Matthew 6:21 and 3 Nephi 13:21: "For where your treasure is, there will your heart be also." As we begin to establish priorities, we should first exercise deep, heartfelt thought. I remember a statement that was taped on our refrigerator when I was a boy: "Far too often we trade the things we want most for the things we want at the moment." Perhaps this is impatience, but it is more likely a matter of heart. It seems that when our hearts are properly focused, we can wait for those things we want most. Elder Russell M. Nelson shared this insight: "When priorities are in place, one can more patiently tolerate unfinished business" ("Lessons from Eve," *Ensign,* November 1987, p. 88).

Elder Boyd K. Packer reminds us that "your responsibility as a father and a husband transcends any other interest in life" (in Conference Report, April 1994, p. 26). We must carefully ensure that our family is a priority of heart. Elder Neal A. Maxwell warns that even good things can obscure our primary priorities: "Sometimes, unintentionally, even certain extra-curricular Church activities, insensitively administered, can hamper family life" (in Conference Report, April 1994, p. 120). A father must establish priorities and then be vigilant. If we don't make a stand for our families, who will?

Honor your priesthood. Review the role of the priesthood, and bring honor to it by your worthiness to bear it. Elder James E. Faust has taught: "The blessings of the priesthood, honored by fathers and husbands and revered by wives and children, can indeed cure the cancer that plagues our society" (in Conference Report, April 1993, p. 47). One way to honor your priesthood is to not only be worthy to bear the priesthood but to use it appropriately. Great strength comes through priesthood blessings. Father's blessings serve as a spiritual legacy within families. Prior to every school year, our family gathers to receive father's blessings, and other significant events always include a fatherly blessing. It is a wonderful privilege to bless the lives of family members through this magnificent power. I must admit that I still seek priesthood blessings from my father and plan to do so as long as possible.

View your life holistically. I am sure you are familiar with the worn cliché, "Home is where you hang your hat." While this statement may suit some, it is grossly inadequate for others. For me, it is a problematic statement. Whenever I hear this cliché, I ask myself, "Which hat?" In our hurried society, we assume so many hats (or roles) that sometimes we almost become split personalities. Granted, the number of hats a father may wear depends upon individual choice, but consider these common hats of modern dads that come in all sizes, shades, and designs: husband hat, father hat, provider hat, Church hat, personal life hat, son hat, sibling hat, neighbor hat, community service hat, and friend hat. According to the cliché, your home is your residence, office, Church meetinghouse, gym, parents' home, cell phone, fax machine, baseball diamond, neighborhood, and friend's den. And you worried that your home wasn't big enough! I am convinced that this is not what the originators of the hat cliché had in mind. Nevertheless, these notions of fragmentation are ingrained in our thinking.

Most people do not view life as a whole. Hence, we feel comfortable talking about our different "hats." We feel that we can take our lives apart as if they are pieces of machinery. We inspect each part, tinker with it, make some adjustments, and then try to reassemble it without affecting the greater whole. Most people divide their lives into neat little pieces or fragments and then try to manage each fragment as if it were a life of its own. We assign each little fragment into a neat compartment. These compartments, fragments, and pieces are the same thing as the "hats" we wear. Soon we begin setting goals for each compartment or hat, such as: wear this hat more often, leave this hat at the office, or get this hat in shape. As we do so, we feel that progress is being made—for the moment.

There are two dangers of fragmentation, both of which brake our progress. The first danger is that fragments *spill over* into each other. Separating hats is not as easy or sterile as one might assume. For example, if we forget to hang our provider hat on the office hat rack when leaving, we usually end up wearing it home. This usually has disruptive consequences because family members generally don't like being treated like employees. President A. Theodore Tuttle said: "It is an unwise father who carries to his family his daily business cares. They disturb the peace existing there. He should leave his worries at the office and enter his home with the spirit of peace in his heart and with the love of God burning within him." ("The Role of Fathers," *Ensign,* January 1974, p. 67.)

Somehow we have forgotten that satisfaction comes when we view life from all angles. Too much emphasis is placed on taking our lives apart rather than letting the whole define the pieces. This leads to the second danger. When we view our lives as separate compartments rather than as one whole, we have a natural tendency to *gravitate* to the compartment where we feel most comfortable or worthwhile. The hat that is most comfortable is the hat we wear most often. If we feel successful and appreciated in our professional role but picked on in our marital role, we will spend more time in the professional compartment and less in the marital and risk developing an attitude of living to work rather than working to live. In time, our professional hat becomes our daily attire for all areas and we become one-dimensional people trying to live a full life. We need to remember that adjustments made in one area greatly influence all the other areas as well.

Administrating versus ministering. With a fragmented perspective, one feels forced to choose between being an administrator or a minister. Rather than being viewed as complementary, these roles become adversarial. As a result we find that fathers are not progressing in their stewardship but regressing to a cardboard cutout of a father. When a father only *manages* his family, family goals, values, and progress tend to be evaluated by bottom-line results. The manager-father feels successful only when he can measure something, such as grade-point averages or the number of touchdowns scored. As with spirituality, however, it is very difficult to measure the visible success of a family. In reality, family happiness has very little to do with measurable things. Joseph and Emma Smith were taught to "lay aside the things of this world, and seek for the things of a better" (D&C 25:10).

A dangerous trend has started in society. Viewing roles as fragments that can be removed or remodeled, society has removed the male responsibility of nurturing and placed it upon those who are deemed better suited for this role: women. Many males feel that it is the woman's role to provide comfort, compassion, solace, and tenderness in the family. Oddly enough both men and women buy into this notion to varying degrees. Society teaches men not to cry during tender situations or allow their feelings to rise close to the surface. Society applauds men who get emotional during sporting events but stand artificially blank when tender moments are at hand. "That's just the way men are," some say. I have been touched by letters written by men during the Civil War, soldiers writing tender, heartrending letters to their wives and children. Men were capable of nurturing in the past, so surely men can take a larger part in that role today. Cheryl Russell feels that the danger in men's modern posture is that "many men are confused about what their role should be, and increasingly, it's no role at all" (*The Master Trend* [New York: Plenum Press, 1993], p. 121). It should be no surprise that within the family unit many men are acting out a worldly concept of family leadership and not exercising true spiritual leadership. Spiritual leadership is not found in the world's models.

Time (not just timing) is of the essence. Whenever the topic of time is addressed in connection with family, two descriptive words are usually used: *quality* and *quantity*. No sane person will argue with the concept of quality time. Obviously making your time with family a quality experience far outweighs any other choice. Sometimes, however, people present the virtues of quality time in a way that causes one to wonder if there are people who actually have difficulty realizing its virtues. It's as if they think a person might say in all seriousness: "I really think my family benefits from my sitting and watching television in my free time. It really builds togetherness."

The problem with the terms *quality* and *quantity* is not with the definitions themselves but with the way the terms are perceived. Quality time and quantity time are almost always perceived as opposites: quality time versus quantity time. This perception seems to imply that if you have a quantity of time it can't be quality time and vice versa. I have often felt that the term "quality time" was invented by those who have very small quantities of time and feel guilty that they are absent so much.

Another myth concerning quality time is the perception that quality use of time translates into doing something. Under this notion, quality time demands action. I am sure we have all experienced meaningful times where there wasn't an agenda. We don't have to schedule bonding time or participate in an activity to feel that we are being together as a family. Some of my most quality family times have been spent lounging in our family hammock and talking about "stuff" with one or all of my family members. It is important to watch clouds float by and use your imagination to describe shapes with younger children. Isn't this quality time? I can even remember when reading the newspaper has been quality time. Reading the newspaper? Quality time? "Surely that is rationalization at its best!" some may argue. But those times when the newspaper is strewn across the floor, with different family members reading their own section lying comfortably on the floor or couch, sometimes have brought our family more togetherness than a planned activity. Granted, there isn't much conversation (usually a quality time must), but we love just being together and having the opportunity to do, or talk, or whatever.

Being in the right place at the right time has always been one of life's difficulties. While timing is of the essence, time is the key. Elder Neal A. Maxwell urged us to "please scrutinize your schedules and priorities in order to ensure that life's prime relationships get more prime time!" (In Conference Report, April 1994, p. 121.) When we think of prime time, the emphasis is usually placed on *prime* rather than *time*. Prime connotes an attitude, a feeling, an emphasis. As a matter of fact, the French and Latin root for *prime* all center around *first*. Perhaps we could view prime time as not just quality time but as time that shows a priority, a choice. We must not just engage in doses of prime time; we must, as Elder Maxwell encouraged, give *"more* prime time."

The realities of providing for family needs are packed with pressure. Providing does require time, and sacrifices have to be made. I remember my daughter being extremely disappointed because I was unable to see her sing at a PTA meeting later one evening. I tried to explain that I had an engagement that I couldn't change with such late notice (I had found out about her program the morning of the performance date). "If you will let me know in advance," I told Megan, "I will do whatever I can to arrange my schedule to make it." Megan was still disappointed, but the incident sparked a remarkable change in our family. Megan made sure I knew ahead of time when parents' visiting day was for her dance class, and I made arrangements to leave early or change an appointment to later in the day. Perhaps the biggest change was that Megan realized that I wanted to be there to support her and be part of the experience. I wasn't choosing to be absent; there were just other commitments of my time. If we can communicate to our family members that they are prime—our first choice, our priority—and if we will arrange to make them come first, it is easier to manage conflicts. When arrangements occasionally cannot be made to attend requested events, understanding can be achieved because we made an effort even if the circumstances prevented any other outcome. There is magic in understanding that you are a priority and not just an afterthought.

Manage your energy. It is ironic that we use the best part of our day doing what is least important to us. Society has it backwards! What would it be like if we worked when we normally would be at home and stayed home when we normally went to work? We would spend all our energy with those who are most important to us and then go to work on half-charged batteries. It is odd that we spend our most energetic time at work and then try to manage meaningful relationships with whatever energy we have left at the end of the day. Most families converge every evening from work, school, and errands feeling hungry, tired, and just plain numb. We can't really change the structure of society, but we can do certain things to manage our low energy levels.

One way to find more energy at the end of the day is to emotionally disengage. This is not a vegetative experience where you lapse into hibernation. Rather, you find something to do that ends the routine of the first part of the day and gives you a fresh start for the next shift. In order to find rejuvenation, some people exercise, go on a walk, or take a shower. While these activities are primarily physical in nature, they can actually rejuvenate you emotionally as well. I believe you can do many things to re-vitalize your emotional energy and get a better start on the second half of the day. I knew a man who played video games when he came home; he called it "mindless stress relief." For me, one of the best ways to end my working day and begin anew is also one of the easiest things: I change my clothes when I come home. It is odd how something so simple makes such a big difference. Per-haps changing clothes allows me to psychologically take off all the emotions from my day and put on a new manner.

Another helpful suggestion is to pay attention to your energy and emotional levels. You should know better than any-one else when your batteries are low or when you are just plain emotionally unavailable. Strangely, however, most people try to hide their fatigue. However, even as we try to be so noble or clever, most family members either recognize the problem immediately or misinterpret our emotional strain. I imagine that many children have grown up thinking their fathers were mad at them when in reality their fathers were just fatigued, worried, emotionally preoccupied, or not feeling well. However, Dad's grunts and mumbling at the dinner table were probably not signs of anger but of emotional release after a hard day. If you share rather than hide your emotional and energy status with members of the family, an interesting experience can occur. Rather than feeling more pressure from family members, you will usually find a support group.

For example, one evening I was sitting at the table eating dinner with my family, feeling physically exhausted and emo-tionally unavailable. I tried to be part of the conversation, but it was obvious that I was not myself. Finally one of the children mustered enough courage to ask, "Are you mad, Dad?" "Mad?" I asked. "Why would you think I'm mad?" As I think back upon this experience, I probably even *talked* in tones that sounded mad. "It's just kinda . . . obvious!" they said. I reassured my family that I was not angry. I told them about my day and the events that had frustrated me. I told them about some of my worries and that I hadn't gotten to bed very early the night before. I wasn't making excuses; I was just sharing my day. Then came the unexpected replies: "Is there anything we can do?" "Are you going to be all right?" "Can I scratch your back?" It was an eye-opening experience as well as an important lesson for the future. There are times when family members want to read a book, go to the store, or do homework with you when you are not available emotionally. Rather than making them feel like you are rejecting them, explain that you are not emotionally available. Ask them to give you some time to gather your thoughts and then if you're able to you'll help. If you explain the circumstances, they will know you are not rejecting *them*.

Be spontaneous. Time management has become a booming industry. I believe there are many advantages in organizing and managing time, but sometimes time cannot be scheduled or controlled. I know many people who get a day planner or organizer to help them run their lives better. They soon find, however, that their planner runs their life rather than vice versa. Some of life's most meaningful experiences are spontaneous. There comes a time when we just put organization aside and let life blossom.

Memorable experiences are often had when routine is broken. Sometimes it is important to stop for ice cream *before* dinner or without a reason. Sometimes children should be allowed to stay up late or have a camp out in Mom and Dad's bedroom. It is okay to let the answering machine take all the telephone calls for the night so that you can concentrate on that Monopoly game. Spontaneity creates a sense of long-lasting excitement within families.

Celebrate. While my wife and I were in Jerusalem, we spent some time at the western temple wall, which is known as the "wailing wall." Here we watched several young men reading from the scriptures as they were initiated into adulthood. I was impressed by how proud their fathers and family members seemed to be. It was a time of celebration that continued in their homes with family and friends.

It is important to celebrate. I am impressed with the Jewish traditions of celebration—feasts, bar mitzvahs, and other traditions. Celebration is not just for having fun; it also deepens meaning. Unfortunately we are usually too busy to celebrate other than on birthdays and holidays. Another important benefit of celebration is that when we celebrate, we reinforce what we believe to be important. For example, it was interesting to compare our experience at the wailing wall with the occasion of a young man receiving the priesthood in his home ward. Both events occur at a similar age. However, I think the young Jewish lad experiences more of a celebration, which helps underline the importance of the event. His extended family gathers, special food is cooked, and festive music is played. The young Mormon boy, on the other hand, is ordained at church and then shakes a few hands and returns home for the usual Sunday dinner. I am not suggesting that we have a festive atmosphere at sacred ordinations; I am, however, suggesting that the attitude of celebration is appropriate and meaningful to such occasions. We should celebrate significant events such as priesthood advancements, Young Women advancements, graduations, engagements, marriages, and births. Whatever we assign as being meaningful in our lives, we should celebrate. Take our family constitution, for example. We wanted our children to understand how meaningful it was, so we framed it and displayed it. Even more important, we declared our own family holiday on the day we signed our family constitution. Once a year, we celebrate that day like any other holiday—the kids even get to miss school!

8

Which Way to Dig?

Many victims caught in avalanches actually survive the initial sweep of the tidal wave of snow. Disoriented and buried, the victims often attempt to dig themselves out. It is not uncommon for rescuers to find that victims have dug in the wrong direction because of severe disorientation. Tragically, some people who are buried in four or five feet of snow tunnel ten or more feet towards the mountain. Thinking they were digging their way to freedom, they were actually burrowing in their grave.

A former professor of mine, Dr. Tom DeLong, related how avalanche disorientation can be prevented and at the same time unwittingly drew a powerful analogy for my life. If avalanche victims would take the time to orient themselves before frantically digging, they would drastically improve their odds for survival. However, when you are covered with snow it is difficult to remain calm and get your bearings. Besides, most people don't know *how* to get their bearings so they can begin digging in the right direction. But there is an accurate way for every person to determine which direction they should dig: simply spit and feel which direction the saliva falls and then dig in the opposite direction.

We have all felt the pressures of life bearing down upon us. Many of us are swept away by mortality's avalanches and end up being buried. Knowing that we are in trouble, we quickly try to dig our way out of our problems. However, mortality has disoriented us, and we usually tend to bury ourselves in more problems rather than uncovering our woes. Taking time to orient ourselves to that which is most important serves as the greatest relief.

During difficult times, when you feel overwhelmed with the rush of life and its demands, when you feel empty even after receiving the world's kudos and praise or just drowned in the world and all its trappings, you can find direction through prayer and listening to divine instruction. I believe Elder Faust was right when he said that "the blessings of the priesthood, honored by fathers and husbands and revered by wives and children, can indeed cure the cancer that plagues our society" (in Conference Report, April 1993, p. 47). Every home should have a priesthood father, and every priesthood father should orient himself according to his divine role. I believe that much of the pressure we feel today is due to the avalanche of mortality. Far too often, we dig ourselves deeper into mortality rather than liberating ourselves from its burdens. The answers are simple: we must start digging, but fortunately we have been instructed, reminded, and encouraged by leaders who have divine perspective of which way is up. Happiness comes to those who understand the simple roles in life.

Once again, I turn to Alma's example with his sons (see Alma 36–42). While society in Zarahemla was unraveling with wars and economic disruptions, Alma turned first to his family and interviewed his sons. In today's similar confusion and social upheaval, fathers must turn back to their families and dig.

Elder A. Theodore Tuttle said: "In the family relationship, we find our best laboratory in which to practice celestial living. While this task is fraught with much challenge and some adversity, it is, nevertheless, blessed with that supreme joy that can come only to a father" (In Conference Report, October 1973, p. 88). For Father's Day one year, my wife gave me a framed saying by an unnamed author that is one of my most prized possessions, for it encompasses a vision reflective of the intent of this book:

> Blessed is the man—
> In whom a clean conscience rests.
> In whom a faithful woman trusts.
> Who finds fulfillment in his work.
> Through whom his children see God.
> In whom good friends comfortably confide.